This book holds a message our cul[...] especially in the age of social media. It's a siren call to set down the measuring sticks and finally learn to say yes to what's right in front of us—the lives we actually have. Sarah is a compassionate guide and honest friend throughout the pages of this book. She leads and teaches from a place of vulnerability but also provides the doses of practicality and thoughtful planning we all need to get unstuck and start moving forward again.

Hannah Brencher, author, *Fighting Forward* and *Come Matter Here*

This is for anyone who has ever felt overwhelmed in this world of comparison and "getting it right." Whether we're struggling in faith or parenting or our own endeavors, Sarah's vulnerability gives space for all of us dealing with comparison and striving and brings hope that we can experience life differently and lean into our unique creativity and experience!

Elizabeth Petters, cohost, the *Deconstructing Mamas* podcast

In *Is Everyone Happier Than Me?*, Sarah Bragg threads the needle on the nuanced complexities of the modern pursuit of happiness, but what makes this reading experience different is the radical authenticity she does it with. Instead of using vapid clichés or vague generalities, Sarah honestly testifies to how both the depression and happiness sausages are made, and we're all the beneficiaries of this cross-examination of the self.

Knox McCoy, author, *All Things Reconsidered* and *The Wondering Years*

I read this in one sitting like a drowning woman clutching a lifesaver. Not only does Sarah Bragg ask all the questions my middle-aged, Gen-X mind obsesses over, but she's also vulnerable about her own struggles and offers ideas for how to help get us off the hamster wheel. *Is Everyone Happier Than Me?* should be handed to every woman as she crosses the threshold of forty. "Happy birthday! Here's your manual. It's gonna be okay."

Melanie Dale, author, *Calm the H*ck Down,*
Infreakinfertility, It's Not Fair, and *Women Are Scary*

Another triumph by Sarah Bragg! Sarah helps us see the sanity, beauty, and authenticity in asking the questions we all have but are not always comfortable bringing to light. Brimming with practical advice, Sarah models for us an authentic life and mature faith. If you feel alone in your struggles, you will find here a trustworthy and wise companion.

Peter Enns, author, *Curveball*

Sarah has taken questions we all ask and methodically unpacked them in her immensely relatable way. Get this book in your library and you'll refer to it often.

Emily Thomas, host, *Struggle Well School*

Sarah's work holds a profound understanding of the dilemmas we face in our daily lives. Her questions are not just inquiries but are tools for introspection and growth, especially for moms juggling the complexities of modern life. I highly recommend *Is Everyone Happier Than Me?* to anyone looking for clarity, connection, and a path to genuine happiness.

Retha Nichole, certified life and business coach

Is Everyone Happier Than Me? is a book I can point clients and friends to as they confront the questions of midlife. Sarah says out loud the things that many of us are afraid to—things we need to talk about that keep us up in the middle of the night. In this refreshingly honest and sharply insightful book, Sarah refuses to leave us alone with our questions. She helps us not only admit our questions out loud but teaches us how to sort through and make sense of them.

Monica DiCristina, MA, LPC

There's not a question in this book I haven't asked myself . . . and often. That's one reason I'm grateful Sarah has chosen to go further than most with her courage to explore rather than suppress hard things. In *Is Everyone Happier Than Me?* you will discover both a relatable companion and a wise friend who serves up some practical life skills. Good for you, Sarah, for helping us all become a little more authentic, kind, and courageous, one honest question at a time.

Kristen Ivy, president and CEO, Orange

is everyone happier than me?

An Honest Guide to the Questions That Keep You Up at Night

Sarah Bragg

ZONDERVAN
BOOKS

ZONDERVAN BOOKS

Is Everyone Happier Than Me?
Copyright © 2024 by Sarah Bragg

Published in Grand Rapids, Michigan, by Zondervan. Zondervan is a registered trademark of The Zondervan Corporation, L.L.C., a wholly owned subsidiary of HarperCollins Christian Publishing, Inc.

Requests for information should be addressed to customercare@harpercollins.com.

Zondervan titles may be purchased in bulk for educational, business, fundraising, or sales promotional use. For information, please email SpecialMarkets@Zondervan.com.

ISBN 978-0-310-36137-4 (softcover)
ISBN 978-0-310-36147-3 (audio)
ISBN 978-0-310-36146-6 (ebook)

Any internet addresses (websites, blogs, etc.) and telephone numbers in this book are offered as a resource. They are not intended in any way to be or imply an endorsement by Zondervan, nor does Zondervan vouch for the content of these sites and numbers for the life of this book.

Published in association with Yates & Yates, www.yates2.com.

Cover design: Micah Kandros
Interior design: Denise Froehlich

Printed in the United States of America

23 24 25 26 27 LBC 5 4 3 2 1

To Scott, my North Star

contents

acknowledgments

Connection. Conversation. Curiosity. Those things are tucked into every page of this book because I have come to value them greatly. As humans, we are wired for connection because connection makes a way for people to feel seen, heard, and valued. Conversation is valuable because it helps us understand others, find next steps, and discover that we aren't alone in the world. And curiosity enables perspective to rise up, conversation to flourish, and judgment to fall to the wayside. This book would not have happened without people who build connection with me, engage in conversation with me, and fuel my curiosity. So, with that in mind, I want to say thank you.

To the readers. We often feel like we're the only one struggling. We wonder if anyone else feels the way we feel. Why is that? I think it's because it's scary to open up, to be honest, to be vulnerable. But we need to be in conversation with each other. We need to open up and be honest. We need to know we are in this together. We need to know we aren't alone. And we need to be curious about life together. So thank you for being in this with me. Thank you for the connection, conversations, and curiosity. I'll share my story so that you will share yours.

To the songwriters who don't know me but speak to me through their music (is it weird to thank famous people who don't know me?): Taylor Swift, Billie Eilish, Olivia Rodrigo, and John Mayer. Keep writing music that makes us feel seen and understood. Thank you for writing songs that connect with me in that way.

To Elizabeth Gilbert for writing *Big Magic*. While I don't know you personally, I want to thank you for being a believer in the creativity that lives in each of us. I reread this book while writing, and it was exactly what I needed to hear. I followed where creativity led, and your book helped push me to keep going and to get out of my own way. Thank you for encouraging me to follow my curiosity.

To the whole Zondervan team—Webb Younce, Paul Fisher, Kim Tanner, Alicia Kasen, Devin Duke, Matt Bray, Bridgette Brooks, and Meaghan Minkus. Thank you for seeing something in me. The creative process is never easy, and I'm thankful for the support you've given along the way. Thank you for making this book better with every hand that touched it.

To my editor, Carolyn McCready. I really appreciate the ease with which you handle the process, your openness, and your desire to let my voice be heard. Thank you for believing in me.

To my agent, Mike Salisbury. Part of why I picked you as an agent is because I could see you as a friend. I genuinely look forward to chatting. Glad I found someone who loves baseball too. I appreciate all your support, confidence, and willingness to go to the mat for me. Thank you for letting me show up as myself.

To my friends. Thank you for all the conversations, texts, calls, and Marco Polo messages while I wrote this book. I would have thrown in the towel many times if I hadn't had your support. During the process, I connected with old friends and made new friends through book clubs, the tennis court, and the gym. Sometimes when you put yourself out there in vulnerable ways (like wearing yoga pants and tank tops while passed out on the mat from too many dead lifts), you find yourself on the receiving end of connection. Thank you for cheering me on.

To Sara Shelton. You have been the greatest gift in this process. I don't think I would have finished the book if it weren't for you. In fact, I can't imagine writing another book without you. You literally carried me across the finish line.

To Scott. You fuel my curiosity more than anyone. I am a deeper thinker because of you. The last two years of pitching and writing this book have been challenging, but you have been by my side through it all—the restless nights and the agonizing mental loops. And even while I don't feel like myself or don't know myself at times (am I a middle schooler?), you have given me constant reassurance of your love and acceptance. Through it all, I feel more connected to you than ever before. Thank you for being with me during the sleepless nights. I love you.

introduction

The Questions We Ask at Night

When my daughter Sinclair was six, she went through a "scared at night" phase. Every night around 1:00 a.m., she would wake up screaming. Why? Because she was terrified or worried about something. Each night the fear was different, almost as if she had a Rolodex she would cycle through.

Tonight I'll be afraid of the dark.

Tomorrow, afraid of burglars.

The next night? Afraid of fire.

Afraid of something in the closet.

Afraid of getting sick.

Afraid of being made fun of at school.

Afraid of a sound I heard.

Night after night, week after week, for almost a year, she repeated this cycle. It didn't take long for my body to anticipate her waking. Each night, I found myself waking around 1:00 a.m., ready for her cry. Her anxiety created anxiety in me. I worried that her scream would wake up her younger sister since they shared a room. So I wanted to be ready, prepared to dash into her room at the first sound of her scream: *"Mom!"*

At the sound of my name, I would throw off the covers and run down the hall to her room. I would quickly open the door and say, "I'm here." In those moments, trying to rationalize with a frightened child doesn't help. All you can do is offer comfort. I would remind her, "I'm here. I'm just down the hall. Your sister is sleeping in the bed next to you. You are loved. You are safe."

Eventually, I could leave her side and crawl back into my bed. Over time, we came up with game plans for all the fears. In the light of day, we tackled the fear of fire. I realized she needed to be prepared. She needed to know we had thought through action steps. We even drew a map together and taped it to the wall by her bed. If she woke up afraid, she still called for me, but we could review the action plan.

That was an exhausting season. I was fatigued. And then that season ended much like the changing of fall to winter. It was over and nearly forgotten.

But then it happened to me.

At some point I created a Rolodex of fears that I cycle through night after night.

I worry about my kids, my husband, my work.

I worry about my weight and berate myself for food or drinks I consumed that day.

I worry about the weather.

I wonder,

Is everyone happier than me?

That's not the only question I ask in the quiet of the night. There's usually a slew of them. Over time, my fears have led to a host of questions that wake me up demanding answers. It seems my mind does its best aerobics at night.

This season of life—midlife, if you will—comes with a lot of feelings, the strongest for me being tired, angry, and unhappy. Many of us have worked at a steady pace for decades at this point, but for what? We seem to end up in a place where we wonder if this is all there is. Those of us born in the 1970s and '80s were the first generation of women to be given a lengthy list of phrases designed to open our eyes to the world of possibility.

You can be anything you want to be.
The world is your oyster.
You can have it all.
You can have the job and raise a family.
You do it all.
You can have a job that you find fulfilling and
    purposeful.

If you're like me, you probably consumed a lot of books and lectures about the importance of finding your passion and purpose. You believed it was all possible, and you bought into the pursuit of it. But where did that leave us? Awake in the middle of the night, questioning it all.

I sat down one day and listed out everything I had felt

over the last several years—a list of the feelings that come with the questions.

lonely	regretful	judged
lost	exhausted	old
invisible	depressed	rejected
bored	unhappy	angry
worried	restless	betrayed
tired	sad	

This list is what inspired me to write the book you're holding now.

I wanted to write a book about this stage of life I'm now in. Not necessarily to try to make sense of it, but at least to let you know you aren't the only one asking the hard questions that come with this season of life; you're not the only one who feels this way.

The irony isn't lost on me that I'm writing about my feelings here. You see, I don't really *like* to "feel my feelings." I would rather acknowledge them, tip my hat to them, and swiftly move on. I think that has a lot to do with my personality and natural wiring.

If you've listened to my podcast, *Surviving Sarah*, then you've likely heard me refer to author Brené Brown as my beloved. Well, back in 2021, my beloved published a whole book about emotions and feelings, titled *Atlas of the Heart*. I read it and was sort of mystified. I remember setting that book down on the coffee table and thinking, "I *know* those feelings, but what am I supposed to *do* with them?"

I wonder if some of my aversion to feelings comes from

the way I was raised. Many of us Gen Xers or even millennials were raised by people whose parents were taught not to express emotions. Or maybe we, especially as women, were told that emotions are a weakness.

Don't show your emotions. Don't be so emotional.

Maybe those of us who grew up in the evangelical church were told that emotions are the opposite of truth. That emotions are essentially bad and can't be trusted. Anytime we felt a negative emotion, we quickly had to dismiss it for fear of sinning. Somewhere along the way, we were told not to believe our feelings.

Don't trust your heart. Don't follow your heart.

It's no wonder that those of us now in midlife don't quite know what to do with all these feelings! It's no wonder we stare at the ceiling at night with a sea of buried emotions and a list of unanswered questions.

What's wrong with me?
Why do I feel so miserable?
Why do I feel so unhappy?

Now I think we need to ask another question: What do I *want* to feel?

I know how I would answer that question. What about you? I think many of our answers would likely boil down to the same thing: We want to be happy.

Happy sort of sums it all up, doesn't it?

I want to feel happy about my stage in life.

Happy about my family.

Happy with what I've accomplished.

Happy with my appearance.

Happy with my relationships.

For me, this search for happiness led to reading a lot of books about the topic. I was curious, of course, to see if there was a specific path to get there and to stay there. Not just to *be* happy but to *remain* happy. I love a good three-step process. I love action. I love for something to boss me around and tell me what to do. Tell me how to not feel this way anymore. So I read the books hoping to come up with a plan.

Do you know what I found? Happiness doesn't look the same to everyone. Happiness isn't a Zen sort of state. Happiness is a feeling, just like all the other ones. It's a feeling indicating my posture toward something or someone in that particular moment or circumstance. It can ebb and flow depending on the season, circumstance, experience, and more. Still, as I read and reflected, I discovered happiness boils down to something common. Something I crave and that has driven me most of my life. Happiness comes down to *connection*. Connection exists between people and carries an energy—like energy running through electric wires—that causes us to feel seen and valued. When connection is formed, it helps us navigate our feelings. Connection is the goal. That's what we crave. Connection is the root of happiness. So instead of pursuing happiness, maybe we should be pursuing connection.

Of course, connection isn't easy, especially in this stage of life. I'm not eighteen anymore. I don't live in a college dorm, spending 24/7 with people. Now connection is much harder to come by. We live in a world where connection seems to be readily available, but it doesn't feel as real as it used to. We're connected through our phones and our online platforms but somehow are more alone than ever.

But if happiness is what we desire and connection is the indicator of it, I decided it was worth the effort to try to find it. Now the question is simply this: How? How do we build connection? How can we become happier? How do we navigate this stage of life, manage the emotions and tensions that come with it, and land in a place where we feel connected not only to others but also to ourselves?

My hope is that in the pages of this book, we both find our answers. To help us get there, I'm going to open up about what I've been feeling. I'm going to tell you the questions I've been asking in the middle of the night. And just as I helped my daughter come up with an action plan during the day to help her in the night, I came up with my own action plan. I'll share what I'm doing to build connection and ultimately find more happiness in my life. This stage of life can be strange and unsettling, but my hope is that if we can speak about it honestly and authentically, then we can find our way together and help each other connect along the way.

is everyone happier than me?

I love music.

It has the power to match your mood or even change your mood.

To me, songwriters and musicians are sort of theologians. They have the ability to communicate thoughts, feelings, and truths in a way we can all understand. A way we can all feel deeply. I remember one of my seminary professors saying that the greatest theologian in any church is the worship pastor. I think that's true. Think about it. You may not remember a word from the sermon your pastor preached on Sunday, but I bet you remember the lyrics to the songs you sang. Why? Because something about the music connected with you on a deeper level. Something about it made you feel something you may not have expected.

That's the power of music.

Of course, musical theologians exist outside the walls of church. I am often moved by lyrics from Taylor Swift, Billie Eilish, and John Mayer. One songwriter in particular played on repeat in our car during the entirety of 2022. It's not just because my girls loved her album; truthfully, my husband, Scott, and I both loved the album too.

The artist? Olivia Rodrigo.

Her debut album, *Sour*, not only captured the angst of adolescence, but I felt like she captured a lot of what us midlifers are feeling too. One of her songs, "Jealousy, Jealousy," has really made me think. If you've never heard it, pause what you're reading and go listen. Trust me, this is important!

Now, here's the gist of the song:

Comparison is killing her slowly.

She thinks too much about people who don't know her.

She's tired of thinking about herself.

Everybody else is getting all the things she wants: vacations, trips, and cool clothes.

If they win, she loses.

If she was just happier or prettier, then . . .

She can't keep up.

Doesn't that song preach?

Please tell me you relate. The feelings she brings to the surface are the ones that plague my thoughts at night. They're feelings that come out to play when I spend too much time and energy in one specific place: social media.

When the internet first became a thing, we all had our rose-colored glasses on. I can't help but think about the movie *You've Got Mail*. We were all Kathleen Kelly opening up an AOL chat, excited to connect. (I'll refrain from now quoting the entire movie to you. If you love that movie, too, then I'm sure you melt at the idea of a bouquet of sharpened pencils.) I think that's where our pull to social media started: with the hope of connection. The internet was the giant wire that could connect you to anyone, anywhere. The world was your oyster. All of a sudden you could find people with common interests somewhere across the globe who may not exist in your area. You could instantly chat with someone about anything at any time. At the beginning, connection seemed easier and more innocent.

But then the internet grew. It evolved and changed. The world got bigger because of it. Now it's more than a connection to friends. We can connect with stores. We can connect with celebrities. We can connect with bots. We can connect with influencers. Bigger and bigger and bigger. More, more, more.

Somewhere along the way, we moved away from the connection we originally hoped we'd find online. Now, instead of being excited to connect, we dread seeing what we don't have. We see an endless feed of luxurious homes, glamorous vacations, beautiful families, fun adventures, massive friend groups, incredible clothes—the list could go on and on. After minutes (or, let's be honest, hours) of endless scrolling, we're left feeling less.

Less connected.

Less secure.

Less of a woman.

Less than.

Eventually, we consider the reality that something must be wrong with us. We wonder why we feel . . .

Jealous.

Envious.

Unhappy.

Judged and judgy.

Self-righteous.

Scroll after scroll, post after post, we're left with the question that keeps us up at night: "Is everyone happier than me?"

I don't know about you, but I don't like feeling that way. Those feelings stir up a lot of angst and leave me depleted. Because those feelings don't stop at Instagram's door, I often drag those feelings into my real-life relationships. After being inundated with how great everyone else's lives appear, I am annoyed by my own. My kids get on my nerves. My husband gets on my nerves. Even my dog gets on my nerves.

Why? Because . . .

I'm jealous of her recent weight loss.

I'm resentful that she keeps finding success and I don't.

I'm embarrassed that my family doesn't seem as with it as theirs.

I'm judgy toward other people for what they think.

I'm self-righteous about what other people do.

No wonder I feel miserable, right?

The thing is, we don't just feel this way because of people we know; even the lives of people we don't know drive our feelings of unhappiness. We look at the lives of celebrities or influencers, and our own lives suddenly seem boring and ordinary. Instead of seeing what we have, we see all that we *don't* have. We're left wondering if our lives would be better—happier—if we had what they have.

If we had a relationship like they have.

If we had kids like they have.

If we had jobs like they have.

If we had popularity like they have.

If we had bodies like they have.

Maybe then we would be happier.

It's a vicious cycle—the kind that keeps me awake at

night questioning every aspect of my life in comparison to the lives I see online.

So if what we see online is driving these feelings, then what are we supposed to do about it? I wish I could throw away my phone, but that's not a legitimate option. How else am I going to find the most efficient way around town? (Hi, I'm Sarah, and I'm addicted to Waze.) Phones are a necessary tool in today's world. We use them to buy our groceries, stay in contact with schools, and even to wake us up each morning. There are endless reasons we need our phones. This is the world in which we live. So how do we navigate it? How do we live here, in the age of social media, and be able to feel anything other than lacking?

To start, let's talk about something we all do.

When I'm faced with what I see online, my go-to reaction (and probably yours too!) is comparison, which causes me to feel jealous, less than, or unhappy.

We have to talk about the elephant in the room if we want to figure out how to move out of our negative feelings and into what we want to feel. We have to address our tendency to compare.

Comparison isn't new. It doesn't exist just because of social media. In truth, we've been reacting this way our whole lives. Research shows that kids begin comparing around the age of five. I know that to be true for myself. A girl called me fat when I was in elementary school, and it was the first time I realized that my body wasn't perfect. I didn't pay much attention to my size until that point. At that point, I realized there was a comparison to be made. Young kids don't know they have that function key. But then their operating system updates with a new feature that enables them to look at someone else, size them up against who they are, and make a comparison about which one is *better*. Note the word *better*. I use that word intentionally. Because at the heart of comparison is competition.

Look at two alike things.

Decide which one is better.

It's important to note how closely linked comparison is to competition. This becomes especially troublesome as we age. We compare our parenting with that of other parents. We compare ourselves with the people who live in our neighborhood, whose kids are on our child's tennis team, or who sit in the pickup line at school. Before social media, we used to leave it at that. Now, though, we have the unique ability to compare our lives with those of people all over the place. We now have the capacity to compete with the entire world. And for someone who loves a good competition, comparison is a dangerous game. I found myself wanting to be the best or have the best or appear the best—no matter what!

Here's the problem: what started as a way to showcase our unique selves has now become a platform to conform to what everyone else is doing. When Instagram launched in 2010, it was a place to highlight your day. People took pictures of what they ate or what was in their line of sight or what they experienced. It felt more like a celebration of photography and the beauty of life, a way to capture in an image something unique to you and your day.

Now it's much more than that.

Nothing has highlighted this change more to me than

the Instagram world of interior design. For a brief moment in my history, I took a stab at helping people decorate their houses. I loved helping them come up with the big picture of how they could make their home feel a certain way. This stint of mine coincided with the introduction of hashtags on the social media platform. With that, you could easily click a hashtag and find similar accounts. In this case, it linked to accounts that inspired your unique design style. You could click a hashtag and scroll through endless pictures that were in the same category. To be seen, you had to constantly create something new. It became a competition to see who could be seen and valued more (more likes equals better).

Just like that, the very first influencers were born. And not only in the world of interior design, but in fashion, kids' birthday parties, family vacations, and much more.

Compare and compete.

Rinse and repeat.

This way of life drains us. It explains why we shut off our phones and feel overwhelmed with sadness, anger, or jealousy. No wonder we struggle to feel gratitude, happiness, and satisfaction. It makes sense that people say comparison is the thief of happiness. It is remarkably easy to feel good about life and then feel the opposite after spending even just a few minutes online. In fact, I hardly remember a time when social media made me feel better.

This is especially true as a content creator. My career as a writer and podcaster requires the use of social media. That is where we all hang out. That is where people are. So if I want you to read what I write or listen to an episode I create, then I must be online. My creative work has to exist in a place where comparison and competition thrive. After years of being on social media, I lost sight of how to create something unique to me. All of a sudden, it became a game to figure out what worked (or more accurately, what was successful) and duplicate it for myself.

The result? My creativity suffered. My creativity was shoved out the door. It all eventually led to the point where I completely avoided being online, taking a much-needed break from consumption.

Compare and compete.

Rinse and repeat.

The day before I turned in my manuscript for my first book, *A Mother's Guide to Raising Herself*, I read a friend's book that had recently released. It was so, so good, timely, and well written. Instead of sitting in that praise for my friend, I immediately thought of my own creative work. Through the lens of comparison, my book felt less than. I immediately questioned what I was about to release into the world.

In hindsight, I know there's space in the world for both our books. Just because her book was so impressive didn't mean my creative work was any less impressive. Her work's greatness doesn't diminish my work. Her creativity doesn't diminish my creativity. We reach people in different ways. We are unique and different. Both beautiful. But in that moment, comparison clouded my eyes with competition. All I saw was the comparison, and it stole my joy about my creative work.

Social media has a way of making us believe that no

matter what we do, we should do it for others to see. We should do it for the praise and response of others. Post the image of our vacation for others. Post an image of our kids for others. Post what I created or wrote for others. Online, we all feel the pressure to be influencers, to earn something from what we create and what we post. Maybe we aim to earn monetary gain, but more simply, maybe we want to earn accolades or likes. We want to earn worth.

Comparison is the thief of happiness because it robs us of connection—connection to ourselves and connection to others. I lost connection to myself when I chose to compare my work with my friend's. I lost sight that I did an amazing thing. Instead, I felt disappointed. And I also lost connection with my friend because I struggled to celebrate and honor what she created.

For me, the biggest trigger of comparison and competition is social media. We show up online to find connection or entertainment, but often we close the device because we feel worse than when we started. We look around and realize we don't have what we want. We see other people experiencing everything we want to experience. Everyone seems happier than we are.

And this isn't just true for us grown-up women. If you are raising teenagers, then you see this playing out in them as well.

Let's talk about social media and kids for a second.

Kids have access to phones earlier and earlier these days. Scott and I were shocked that nearly all the kids in our daughter Rory's fifth-grade class already had phones. We felt like we were the lone holdouts because our kids were in middle school without phones. Sinclair finally received a phone at the end of eighth grade. She got social media at age fourteen upon entering high school. And even that age felt too young to me.

Young brains aren't developed enough to handle the complexities of social media. As someone in my midforties, I know that social media is someone's highlight reel. And that it's a place where companies go to sell their products. Even though I know that, I still struggle not to compare and compete. Yet we allow our kids to play there?

I've heard we need to model how to handle social media for our kids, but if I'm honest, I don't feel fully competent in that, and my brain is fully developed! If it's dangerous for us to play there, then it's even more dangerous for our kids. It's difficult for them to see the comparison trap.

Move On and Let Go

Finally, I hit my personal breaking point. I wanted to lessen whatever was driving comparison and pulling me away from connection and creativity. I wanted to remove the source of my negative feelings like self-righteousness, jealousy, and angst. I didn't want to feel those negative thoughts every time I opened my social media accounts. I wanted to see if there was a way to feel creative again, to

I wanted to see if there was a way to feel creative again, to see if there was a way to enjoy my life and create something—even if nobody else saw it or gave it a like.

11

see if there was a way to enjoy my life and create something—even if nobody else saw it or gave it a like.

Can I tell you the final straw that made me take a break from social media? It was a parade. Not just any parade, though. It was the parade that celebrated the Atlanta Braves World Series victory. We lived about fifteen minutes from the Braves stadium, and when we moved to Tennessee, leaving the Braves was at the top of the con list. Attending games was a big part of our family's life. I knew we couldn't attend the parade now that we lived in a different state, and I felt intense jealousy toward all the people I knew who would attend.

Even though that was a petty, childish reason to avoid social media, it was motivation to take a break. I knew that nothing good would rise up in my heart by being online during that time. I committed to not checking social media for forty-eight hours. Two days turned into a week, and before I knew it, I was on a break from social media. The Braves parade (petty or not) was the motivation I needed to start.

Initially, it was shocking how many times I went to open that app. Without me even thinking about it, my fingers would magically return to where it once lived on my phone. After some time, I opened the app again so I could check my messages. I hated the thought of people feeling like I was ghosting them if they contacted me. I put the app in a folder on the farthest screen from my home screen. I allowed myself to check messages once a day. I would open the app and then literally use my left had to cover all the images and stories so that I could see only my messages. I didn't want to get back on the comparison-and-competition ride.

I lived social media free for four months.

Let me tell you. Those were some great months. I had more time on my hands. Instead of endlessly scrolling, I played solitaire on my phone when I got bored. (It's not lost on me that I was going to Instagram because of boredom.) Doing something like that helped me take a baby step away from social media. Sure, I was still on a screen, but solitaire didn't cause me to compare and compete. I leaned into creativity. I purchased a guitar. I played the ukulele. I bought a hand-lettering guidebook. Not only that, but I got active. I started walking again. (If you've read *A Mother's Guide to Raising Herself*, then you know I call my daily walks smoke breaks. Don't worry—there's no actual smoking involved!) I worked in our pasture shoveling poop. It wasn't glamorous, but it was gratifying—I was doing something. I was accomplishing something. (Scrolling social media didn't really accomplish much.) I started reading more fiction. Instead of sitting on my phone during the afternoon carpool, I read a book. (You'd be surprised how many books I was able to read during that time away from social media.) I reached out to a friend, and we started going for coffee every week, talking face-to-face instead of typing words on a screen, and wandering around antique stores.

All of these things were beneficial.

All of these things inspired me.

All of these things left me feeling better instead of worse.

I want the same for you. I'm not saying you should throw your phone in the water or take a four-month fast from social media. The how may look different for you than it did for me. But we all need to find a better way to show up online. We need to find ways to foster creativity and connection in real, everyday life. And we need to try to replace those feelings of jealousy, anger, and judgment with happiness, connection, and creativity.

So what do we do? How do we let go of comparison? What should we lean in to in its place?

For starters, we need to acknowledge that the inclination to compare is normal and human. If you are breathing, then you will compare. We can't do anything to prevent that from happening. You may not be able to stop yourself from comparing, but you can choose whether to let that comparison affect your mood and your self-worth. That is the key.

When you feel the rinse and repeat rise up—*Are they happier than me?*—pay attention. Before falling down the rabbit hole of comparison and angst about your life, stop and choose differently. The answer comes down to choosing to change your perspective. Their life doesn't have to negatively affect your life. When I see others' posts, I'm working on saying, "Good for you." Not in a sarcastic way but in an honest way.

Trip to the Bahamas. *Good for you.*

Kid getting all the blue ribbons. *Good for you.*

Smiling family. *Good for you.*

Gorgeous new house. *Good for you.*

A bajillion followers. *Good for you.*

Simply acknowledge the good that someone else has. Doing this doesn't take away from the good that you have. Their value has no effect on your value. Acknowledge their life, wish them well, and move on. And if that doesn't work?

If you still struggle to wish them well, if you still struggle not to feel anger, resentment, or frustration? Then set up a guardrail. Maybe you could simply mute them. I think that's the modern-day way of guarding your heart. You don't have to unfollow or unfriend. Simply mute them. Muting serves as an effective guardrail. I fully recognize that comparison doesn't limit itself to online relationships. Comparison rises up just as easily in real-life relationships. Guardrails are needed there too. You can't easily mute those people, but you can create distance if needed. Sometimes time away lessens the urge to compare, but sometimes we have to do the hard thing of saying, "Good for you." Even if you don't say it out loud, the internal practice is still helpful.

Simply acknowledge the good that someone else has.

Remember, you have the choice to let go of comparison and move on.

The Antidote to Comparison

Guardrails and the phrase "Good for you" can be helpful to working through the negative emotions around comparison, but there's another helpful antidote to consider. Cultivating creativity can go a long way in countering the tendency to compare. Brené Brown said, "Creativity, which is the expression of our originality, helps us stay mindful that what we bring to the world is completely original and cannot be compared. And, without comparison, concepts like ahead or behind or best or worst lose their meaning."[1] So much creativity is packed inside you. It's what makes you original—what makes you, you. And tapping into that creativity can be integral to your happiness.

Until recently, I had never made the connection that creativity helps combat comparison. Maybe that's a new revelation to you too. Think about it in regard to children and what they create. A healthy childhood is nearly defined by creativity, from the art they make to how they dress themselves to what they play. We encourage kids' creativity. We see it as essential to their well-being.

My girls are older now, but I have a box filled with their art projects and creations from when they were younger. All my bookmarks are ones the girls made out of notecards. When my girls create something, do I immediately compare it with something else? With someone else's creation? No. Why? Because it is theirs. It's original. No other story is exactly like Sinclair's *Donutlandia*. No other handprint "turkey" was made with Rory's hand. Their art is unique to them.

Creativity can be shared publicly or not, but if you share online, share with some level of caution. Wanting your art to be seen isn't a bad thing. My girls used to jump up and down to show me what they created. Even now they are excited to see my smile when they present any work of their own hands and imagination. I feel the same about what I create. I want to share what I create with others, much like my girls do. But I do so carefully, knowing I will have to fight hard against comparison.

Creativity is about being unique, while comparison

is about competition. Comparison is about conforming to what other people are doing and trying to do it better. When I stepped back from social media, I gave myself space to be creative without feeling the pressure to share my content online. Creativity without competition allowed me to be inspired again. I was able to stop worrying about how my art was received. It gave me space to stop obsessing over what others were doing, hitting the numbers, measuring up, or whether I was "winning." Stepping away from social media allowed me to do something that was just for me. It allowed me to connect to myself—to what I found inspiring, interesting, fun. And I was able to connect with others from a place of happiness for them because I wasn't focused on how I compared. To feel more happiness, we need to cultivate our creativity.

Drop the Measuring Stick

In our letting go of comparison, we also need to develop self-compassion and self-acceptance. Comparison does not cultivate self-acceptance, belonging, or authenticity. Instead, it makes us judge our creative selves and feel like we don't measure up. We try to copy what someone else is doing because what they're doing is "working." We conform and settle for fitting in instead of being truly known for who we are. And listen, I get it. Being honest about who we are is scary, especially online, where people we don't even know feel that they can comment on and critique everything we say, do, or post.

To stay online yet free from comparison, we have to put away the measuring stick. Resist the urge to compare. Show compassion and acceptance toward yourself with what you create. When I was struggling, I found it hard to show up online in a way that felt authentic. Posting about ideas I was thinking about or stories about our life seemed too vulnerable at the time. I felt like if I shared, it would only be because I was staring at a measuring stick between me and someone else in the same field of work. So instead, I shared pictures of our horses. No commentary. Just what my eyes saw daily. And when I shared, I would remind myself that what I do or don't do is okay. I worked to show myself compassion and acceptance.

The more we practice dropping the comparison stick, the less we will succumb to the pressure to compare and compete.

Created to Create

Engaging in creative outlets is proven to improve your brain function, mental health, and physical health. Have you ever noticed a difference in your mood when you do something as simple as listening to music while cleaning or cooking? Or when you were bored as a child, what did you do? When you had to sit in church or take a long car ride or listen to a teacher's lecture, did you draw or doodle? I always did. I have many pages with my name written in bubble letters or with little drawings scattered along the margins. That's creative work. These sorts of activities give our brains space to sort out our thoughts and feelings. So when we are knee-deep in the comparison trap, trying to do something creative makes sense. Because being creative taps into the very essence of being human. We are all creative beings. The creation story in the Bible describes a creative God—just look at the description of all that was dreamed up and created: stars, water, night, day, vegetation. Reading that story paints a picture of artistry in our minds. If God is creative and we were made in his image, what does that say about us? We are created to create.

Good news: this is not a one-size-fits-all scenario—you can do anything creative here. Activities like knitting, drawing, coloring, cooking, and writing are repetitive in nature and produce a visible result. And what happens when you see the result? Your brain is flooded with the feel-good chemical dopamine. When you feel dopamine, you feel more motivated. You feel happier.

So when you find yourself stuck in the comparison trap, take action. Do something creative. Journal about it. Paint something. Put on some music and dance. That creative motion will help you work yourself out of the trap.

While we would ideally avoid the comparison trap, fully avoiding it is unlikely. But we can be aware that it exists. And because we know it exists, we must be mindful of what triggers us, of the places or people that tend to draw us into the trap, and then avoid them as needed.

Maybe that looks like taking a break from social media like I did. Or maybe it means setting a timer. We have app limits set on our girls' phones. At this moment, only Sinclair has social media, and we've limited how many social apps she can have. And we limit how long she can use each app. We set those time limits on her phone so it will shut off when her time is up. Maybe this is something we need to consider for ourselves. Now that I'm back on social media, I can feel the lure of comparison. I once again find myself endlessly scrolling. So I recently set a time limit. After thirty minutes a day on Instagram, the app shuts off. This is a boundary that keeps me from falling into the soul-sucking comparison trap once again.

Maybe removing the app or setting time limits isn't helpful for you. Let me give you one other suggestion. When you feel unhappy, go back to your photos *stored on your phone*. Scroll past the random pictures of receipts or parking spots (tell me I'm not the only one who forgets where she parks). Just look at all those pictures. Those pictures are of people and places that brought you happiness. Even the hundred photos of your daughter's face when she stole your phone and snapped 0.5 selfies. Just look at her face! No one takes photos and videos of life sucking. No one takes a photo of the tragic state of their pantry. No one wants to commemorate the stuff that makes them feel the worst. When you feel unhappy, go look at your phone's photo library and smile. Feed yourself something other than what's on social. Look at your photos—your life—instead of someone else's.

And lastly, when we feel the urge to compare and compete, we need to learn to celebrate. Nothing kills comparison faster than celebration. The very act of celebrating someone else takes us out of our own heads, where comparison wants to keep us.

For decades, I have worked on cultivating celebration. I

like to describe it as throwing confetti. Of my girls, Rory is the one who has picked up on the same level of celebration. She loves a party. She will plan her birthday eight months in advance. And when she's invited to parties, she is thoughtful about the presents she gives. When she was little, every party she attended, she positioned herself right next to the guest of honor. She would look at her friend and grin ear to ear. That's the picture of celebrating that I have in my mind. When I see someone getting accolades for something they did, or getting the home they always dreamed of, or getting their book published, I want to be like Rory. I want to sit beside them and grin ear to ear. I want to throw confetti and celebrate the good they are experiencing—even if I'm not.

Nothing kills comparison faster than confetti.

So when you lay awake at night and wonder if everybody's happier than you, remember that everyone is on their own journey. My friend Ashley always used to say, "That's *their* journey." Just because that's their journey doesn't mean it needs to be your journey. Just because their journey includes a vacation home doesn't mean that should be your journey. Just because their journey includes raising kids doesn't mean that should be your journey. Just because their journey includes striving for a particular something doesn't mean that should be your journey.

> Nothing kills comparison faster than confetti.

Remember that you are doing what you are doing in life because you enjoy it. You were interested in it or you loved

2
CHAPTER

will i always feel stuck?

I remember my first encounter with a chart and gold stars.

I grew up going to First Baptist Church. Baptist churches in particular were all about offering ways to learn more about the Bible. Along with weekly Sunday school, other classes were always happening at the church, one of those being Bible Drill. The point of Bible Drill was to get kids to memorize Bible verses. Every week, each kid would recite the verse they had memorized. With each successful recitation of a verse, a gold star was placed on a handmade poster board chart.

I'm convinced that Bible Drill was created for kids like me. Those who are competitive and motivated by achievement. Those who crave the satisfaction of seeing the gold stars appear beside their name on the chart.

Yes, I was one of those kids. Truth be told, I'm probably one of those adults too.

Not to brag, but I was the best. Okay, I'm full-on bragging. I was even state champ! (No, no, I am not ashamed to admit that. I still take great pride in those gold stars.)

My striving for gold stars didn't end there. I've worked for those stars my whole life. They obviously came in different shapes and forms once I got past childhood. No one in adulthood is putting stickers on a chart. Getting gold stars sometimes looks like health apps where you track what you eat and if you've been "good" you might get shooting stars or fireworks or complete your circle. WeightWatchers will even send you a little purple tag for your key chain to celebrate your progress (hello, gold stars!). And climbing the corporate ladder can be like raking up gold stars. My husband, Scott, has often said I would have thrived in the corporate world. Clearly, he's seen firsthand my love for gold stars. Getting gold stars can look like reaching a marriage milestone. Married for ten years, fifteen years, twenty years. Gold stars! Or maybe it looks like finally getting out of debt or being able to buy a house. Maybe it looks like getting a gold star for raising a kid who receives gold stars.

Honestly, there's a thrill that comes with achievement.

Years ago, when podcasts were new-ish and I launched *Surviving Sarah*, one of the greatest things that could've happened for the show was to land on the iTunes New and Noteworthy list. Podcasters didn't have a lot of control over getting on the list. The achievement was based on a mix of number of downloads and number of reviews. I still remember pulling up iTunes and seeing *Surviving Sarah* sitting on the New and Noteworthy list. It was a rush to see my show there! My girls, who were young at the time, equated me with Taylor Swift. Taylor is on iTunes. Mom is on iTunes. Same, same. It felt like gold stars to me.

Gold stars are all fun and dandy . . .

Until you stop progressing.

Until you stop receiving those rewards.

Until you stop achieving.

Until you get stuck.

All of a sudden you realize you've been working hard toward a goal, but the goal keeps feeling further away. You've been trying to lose weight, but nothing has happened on the scale. You've been trying to grow your business, but the numbers aren't improving. You've been "doing all the right things" to help your child develop into a healthy functioning human, but they don't seem to listen to or heed your advice. Your marriage starts to struggle after all these years. The market tanks and you can no longer afford the house you had been saving for. Nothing seems to be progressing, and everything feels stuck.

This happened to me in the summer of 2021. This wasn't the first time I'd felt stuck, and it certainly won't be the last. By midsummer that year, I hardly recognized myself. I had most certainly gained the "COVID-19" in pounds (similar to the "freshman fifteen" but with a much slower metabolism than I had at eighteen). Up until that point, I had mostly just complained about it. I grumbled and grumbled about my clothes not fitting. I griped about the extra weight. I bemoaned my body image. But that's where it ended. By that summer, I finally felt like it was time to do something about it. I was ready to set a goal and make some progress. Somebody create the poster board and get the gold stars—I had work to do!

I contacted my friend who's a trainer, and we made a plan. I started working out with her in studio twice a week. This was a big step because I felt embarrassed about my appearance. I used to be a college athlete, for crying out loud! Now I was a washed-up fortysomething who got winded easily during a workout.

Still, I pushed through. I could see those gold stars waiting to be given. After three months of working out together, my friend and I stopped to reassess. We measured my progress. Standing on the scale, I could practically hear the applause for the work I'd put in. Move over, Bible Drill, because there was a new competition I was about to win!

Except I didn't. Would you believe that I didn't lose any weight? Rather, I gained four pounds! Sure, I gained some muscle weight, but because I had lived my whole life in accordance to the numbers on the scale, those extra pounds were devastating.

You don't want to know the words shouting in my mind when I saw those results. I definitely didn't get any gold stars. No progress. No achievement. No rewards for my effort.

In my mind, it was all failure.

To say I felt defeated would be an understatement. After all that work, all that dedication, all that showing up when I didn't feel like it—and nothing. I thought I was progressing, but all I felt in that moment was stuck. And I wondered,

Will I always feel stuck?

This sort of thing happens in other areas of our lives too. A lack of progress in work or life or relationships can leave us feeling defeated. And feeling defeated leaves us feeling stuck, unsure of how to move forward, fearful that we can't move forward.

I've had many conversations with women just like us. I'm not sure if that's good news or bad news; maybe it's just life. Either way, trust me when I tell you that we aren't the only ones who are unsure about how to move forward. We aren't the only ones who feel sad because we aren't progressing the way we hoped. We aren't the only ones who think we might be stuck.

When we feel like we aren't making progress, it's important to take note of what might be getting in the way. I'm sure you could tell me a number of reasons you think you might be struggling. In my conversations with others like us (and in my self-exploration of trying to get myself unstuck), I've found it usually comes down to a few similar themes.

Perfectionism

The first (and probably most prevalent) reason we feel stuck? Perfectionism.

Progress feels like forward motion, and forward motion in life is a powerful thing. Even the smallest steps forward can be motivating enough to keep us going. Those small steps can feel like jet fuel at times. But the one thing that can stop my forward motion in its tracks is my desire for perfection.

Perfectionism tells us there's one way to do something—the perfect way to do something. When we have that mentality and face an obstacle, we feel defeated. Why? Because we think that if we didn't do something perfectly, we failed. End of story. Now what?

In my dealings with perfectionism, I've learned that it's really about trying to protect myself. I can see this in my little-kid self, chasing those gold stars for memorizing Bible verses. Sure, she wanted to win, but more than that, she didn't want to fail. She was vulnerable enough to put herself out there and try to recite those verses from memory yet perpetually afraid that her vulnerability would be for nothing. For her, perfectionism was an armor. And while I wish I could say I outgrew that armor, the reality is that I brought it with me into the midlife years. It's my defense mechanism when I feel threatened, afraid, or on the verge of failure or shame. If I can just look perfect, do perfect, be perfect, then I can avoid shame, judgment, and blame. I can stay protected.

One of the easiest places to see perfectionism as a means to self-protect is with diet and exercise. I hadn't realized before how much I was driven by perfection. When it came to dieting and exercising, it couldn't be two steps forward, one step back. At least not for me! For me, it had to be perfection because perfection equaled worth. If I didn't perfectly follow my diet plan or hit my desired number of steps every single day, I thought I failed. I felt shame.

It was the need for perfection, not the numbers on the scale, that ultimately impeded my progress. If my steps weren't perfectly executed to take me to my goal in the time and manner I wanted, then it simply wasn't success. And that mindset impacted my ability to see that *progress is success*. This need for perfection shows up in many areas of my life. It shows up in frustration over the clothes I wear or the way my hair looks. It shows up in my career—needing to look like I'm doing better than maybe I really am. It shows up in my family—thinking there is a right way to be a family and feeling shame when reality doesn't match up to that picture.

Maybe you can relate.

When you feel vulnerable, uncertain, or afraid, do you put on perfection as an armor?

Does your pursuit of perfection diminish your enjoyment of life?

Has perfectionism hindered your progress?

If this is our reality, how do we let go? How do we get unstuck from the need for perfection and allow ourselves to be in process in order to make progress?

Here's the good news: awareness is half the battle! Simply acknowledging your desire for perfection is a huge step. Because once you know it, you can see it. When it comes to letting go of perfection, you have to pay attention to how that desire shows up. I can trace back the self-protection of perfectionism all the way to those gold-star days of Bible Drill. I was afraid of not being loved or valued. Even as a child, I thought performance was the key to being loved. I still struggle with that belief, so I have to pay attention when I feel myself putting on my armor, starting to self-protect.

The next time you notice a desire to be perfect, stop and pay attention. Be curious about what's motivating your pursuit of perfection. What is lurking below the surface? Remember, perfectionism is a defensive mode, so check whether your desire is about improving yourself or protecting yourself.

Remember, perfectionism is a defensive mode, so check whether your desire is about improving yourself or protecting yourself.

Let's go back to the health and fitness example. I've already alluded to the fact that perfectionism motivated the entirety of my personal health and wellness journey up to that point in my life. Perfectionism is others focused. In other words, it asks, *What will people think? Will I look good in photos? Will people think I look good in my clothes?* That kind of perfectionism is about perception, which is something I ultimately can't control.

When I stood on that scale a few months after beginning to work out, I wanted to quit. To run away. To throw in the towel and call it a day on this health and wellness journey. That's not a healthy response to struggle, is it? Well, don't worry—that's not what I did. Though what I did instead wasn't much better. I dug my heels into perfection. I downloaded a weight loss app. I tracked my food like a hawk. And you know what happened? I lost weight. Striving for perfection to protect myself from shame paid off.

Until it didn't.

It wasn't one month after reaching my goal weight that I turned around and put five pounds back on. Six months later, another five pounds. Abruptly, I was right back where I started. I felt terrible. I felt ashamed. I felt exposed. I felt defeated.

I felt stuck . . . again.

My desire for perfection inhibited my ability to celebrate my progress, which I made a lot of in that season. It just wasn't the progress I was hoping for. I was focused on the number on the scale, which showed a lack of progress. What I didn't realize was that progress looked like signing up to go to the gym. Progress looked like showing up twice a week to work out. Progress was simply caring enough to keep going. To get unstuck, I needed to shift my perspective so I could celebrate the small moments of progress, not just the end result of perfection. I needed to remember that it was more important to focus on improving my habits, my health, and my life, and not on what others would think.

I recently sat on my therapist's sofa peeling back the layers of why I have such angst about my appearance and performance. I talked about the freedom I might feel if I just let myself do the hard work of deconstructing my worldview regarding worth. I finally told her that I'm afraid of being free because that might mean being heavier on the scale.

She asked me to be honest—really honest—about what I was afraid of in this specific scenario.

Honestly?

Afraid of being unseen.

Afraid of being ordinary.

Afraid of being uncool.

My perfectionism in the areas of appearance and performance has been a mode of self-protection my whole life. And now, that self-protection was keeping me from getting unstuck. I couldn't see the progress I was making. I couldn't see that, in many ways, I was earning little gold stars for my efforts each day. Simply trying was a step toward success, but perfection said that wasn't enough.

Once I reframed the way I saw my efforts in working out in that season, I saw progress. I started to feel free. I started to get unstuck. Let me be clear: the number on the scale hasn't changed. That outcome hasn't been reached, and while that reality isn't always easy to accept, it is okay. Because now I see progress over perfection.

Brain Space

Sometimes you can't make progress in one area because your mind is overrun in just about every other area. I've always had a little trouble making mental space to tackle what's in front of me, but this struggle has become even more pronounced since I became a mom. Many plates are spinning at any given moment. Making sure people eat three meals a day requires mental effort. Coordinating schedules can cause blood pressure to rise. Managing all the emotions sometimes feels like a full-time job. With all that on the brain, it's no wonder we feel so overwhelmed that we can't seem to create forward motion.

In 2021 it was time to write this book. The problem? I was overwhelmed. We had just moved from Georgia back home to Tennessee, and the honeymoon phase of the move was over. All the stress of moving had caught up to me. Reality was setting in.

We had lived nearly eight years—my girls' formative years—in Marietta. We had built a good life there. And now, nearly a year after moving, my heart felt the weight of leaving. I missed our life there. Every day, keeping everything going felt like work. It was hard to keep pace. Adjusting took a lot of effort. We had to adjust to two new schools for the girls, and middle school was hard.

Yet I was supposed to start writing another book. I just couldn't imagine having the mental space to write anything worthwhile. My mind was taxed and overrun. How was I supposed to find words of help and encouragement for others if I couldn't find them for myself? How could I be everyone's cheerleader when I struggled to be my kids' cheerleader?

The overwhelm left me stuck. Knee-deep kind of stuck.

To get unstuck, I again had to focus on progress rather than perfection. Progress looked like taking note of where I was mentally. Progress looked like quieting my mind enough to figure out what I needed. Progress looked like making space—not just mental space but physical space in my schedule.

I kept my other part-time work because we still needed my income, but I pressed pause on the podcast and my writing. For a long time I focused only on the necessities. I focused my energy on what I needed and what my family needed. Time to take walks and to work on my house. Time to have coffee with people. Time to be with my parents now that I lived next door to them. Time to be present with my girls when they arrived home from school.

I narrowed my focus and made space for what I needed most in that season. And I did just that until I had space in my mind for more. Over time, I felt the urge to write again. How did I know? I knew because words were coming to mind. As I walked, inspiration was striking again. I could tell I was ready to write because desire was bubbling up inside me. Do you see that connection? My brain needed space. Sometimes our brains can only do so much at a time. The physical and mental space allowed my brain to spark creativity again. Even as I write, my capacity to do all that I was doing hasn't returned, but progress has been made.

I had the same conversation with two different friends over the course of the last year, each one wanting to make progress with their health and each one in the middle of major hardship because of change. I told them the same thing I told myself in that season: When the dust settles, then you can make space for progress. Sometimes one thing has to end to free up brain space for something else.

But freeing up this kind of space is a lot easier said than done.

In 2009 a UCLA study found that women's stress levels are directly proportional to the amount of stuff in their homes.[2]

I know that's true. How do I know? Because if there is one thing that can send me into beast mode—turning me from a happy-go-lucky mom to an everyone's-going-to-die mom—it's *stuff*. I have a pretty good handle on the stuff that is in 75 percent of the house. We live in a two-story family home, and the layout essentially gives our girls the run of the upstairs. Up there, they have two bedrooms, one bathroom, and a common space. Upon writing these words, I have been banned from entering said domain. To be clear, my kids didn't ban me; they don't have that power. Scott, however, does. And that's who issued the banishment. Why? Because walking into that space for me is like walking into a dystopian world.

There is stuff *everywhere.*

Random socks scattered throughout? Check.

Last night's snacks? Check.

Last week's snacks? Check.

Glasses with milk remnants inside? Check.

Paper and trash all over the floor and every surface? Check and check.

Seeing the mess always leaves me stressed and angry. Reading that study about how our stress is connected to the clutter in our homes affirmed what happens every time I enter their space. Clutter can affect our anxiety level, our sleep, our focus. That last one is especially true for those of us who already struggle to find enough brain space. The clutter on the outside can create clutter on the inside, making us feel less and less productive.

If you can relate, let me give you something to try.

After Christmas last year, my brain felt especially cluttered. To clear my mind, I first had to clear up my clutter. I tackled one drawer at a time. I bought pretty little clear organizers (thank you, The Home Edit, for your constant inspiration) and started making space. Did it solve all my problems? Not at all. But making space physically brought me space mentally. So if you're not sure how to make space in your mind, start by making space in your space.

If we can give ourselves gold stars each time we choose to pause long enough to clear our heads and tackle the tasks we need to, that's progress. And that's worth celebrating.

Goals

If we're going to talk about progress, then we also have to talk about goals.

I've never been one to set goals (unexpected from an Enneagram 3, I know!). I would much rather achieve something and then retrospectively set the goal. That way I only set goals that I achieve (I should talk about that in therapy).

I probably do this because I don't like to fail. I don't like to let anyone down (including myself!).

As I write this chapter, the calendar has turned to a new year. Everywhere I look, people are posting about goals for the coming year. Even though I don't like goals, I'm tempted to succumb to peer pressure and try to think of some goals to achieve. I do love the idea of new pages and fresh starts, but the transition to a new year carries a lot of pressure.

Pressure to do it differently.

Pressure to see progress in big, obvious ways.

Pressure to achieve it all.

Pressure to reinvent yourself.

New year, new you, right?

What I've come to realize is that reinventing myself in a calendar year is an impossible task. Most of the changes in me have happened over time. Not just days, months, or even one clean calendar year, but *years* of progress.

In the early days of 2023, I looked back through my journal to the year before. One entry was dated January 3, 2022. No specific goals were listed, but what I read revealed the mental state of my being.

I feel hopeless about my weight. I keep trying. I set the goal with a new plan. But I feel stuck. The scale isn't moving.

I had so much anxiety in the night. Worried about my book. Worried about my weight. Worried about how much screen time the girls have. Worried about their future.

The woman who wrote those words a year ago was stressed to the max. Her anxiety level was clearly through the roof. In short, she was miserable.

As I read my words from the start of the previous year, I realized I didn't want to feel that way anymore. I wanted to accept who I am while working to take care of my body. I wanted to keep working out. I wanted to keep choosing moderation in regard to food. But I didn't want misery to motivate those choices. That's when it hit me that maybe my slogan should be:

New year, same Sarah, but different.

In other words, there would be no reinventing. There would just be progress.

Because, like I said, there's value in progress. It's what helps us get unstuck. It's what's at the heart of the goals we set every time a new year starts. We all want to make progress in life. And setting goals can help us make some much-needed

T here's value in progress. It's what helps us get unstuck.

progress. But goals based on wrong motives? There's little real or helpful progress to be found there.

When I felt so miserable about my body and started working out, I did so with a goal in mind. I wanted to lose weight. I wanted my clothes to fit. I wanted to see a certain number on the scale. When I read through my journal, I saw that I lost five pounds in two weeks. I could hear the lift in my voice as I wrote about it. Progress was pulling me forward, but I couldn't celebrate or even acknowledge it because I hadn't hit my goal.

There had to be a shift, not in the goals but in the motivation behind them.

I also applied this principle to my writing of this book. Each time I sat down at the computer, I saw progress in my writing. With every day I wrote, the number of words increased. Now, these words may not have been any good initially, but that's okay. Ultimately, my goal in writing this book was simply to show up, be honest, and make progress. With that perspective in mind, I felt better. I felt less stuck.

There is something powerful about progress.

A word of caution here: we have to be careful with our goals. We have to be wary of becoming so ambitious that we set goals we can't achieve. For my fellow achievers out there, this one isn't easy. It's in our nature to chase, to pursue, to get the gold stars, even the ones that are impossible to reach. I speak from experience when I tell you that approach doesn't leave you any less stuck than when you started.

Years ago, I started reading a book about completing goals by Jon Acuff called *Finish*. Ironically, I never finished the book, but one piece of advice stuck with me. He said to cut your goals in half. For example, if you want to lose ten pounds, set a goal for five pounds. If you want to read two books a month, set a goal for one book a month. In my effort to escape the sense of failure that comes with writing, I applied his method to this book. At first I set a goal for five thousand words a week. Then I cut it in half. This simple change made the writing feel more manageable. It made the goal feel achievable.

Making changes or improvements will require making better choices. Each choice is a form of progress! One choice at a time, over time, will lead to real changes and to getting unstuck. I set more achievable goals for my writing, yes, but daily I had to choose to show up and write. Then when I hit the goal for the day, I got to make another choice: keep going or find the freedom to walk away. Either way, I had made progress. I wasn't stuck.

The same can be true for you! Allow yourself the freedom to take time—one choice at a time—to work toward your goal. Then do it again the next day. Pay attention to the little tasks you accomplish. Celebrate the small steps of progress. Revel in the freedom of being unstuck.

A Work in Progress

I often berate myself because I should be further by now. I should be faster at something. I should have it figured out. I should have more gold stars racked up beside my name.

But the biggest hindrance to seeing results isn't that I'm not trying. It isn't that I'm not tracking my food accurately. It isn't that I'm not showing up enough. The biggest hindrance is my mindset. I am my own worst enemy. I am the nagging voice in my head saying that I'm not doing it right or well enough. That I can't do it perfectly. That I won't reach my goals. That I'll never find the space to make any sort of forward progress.

Dear reader, you are a work in progress.

What would happen if I reminded myself of this same truth?

I'm a work in progress.

Reader, we're all a work in progress. And that means...

It's okay to be where you are.

It's okay to still be working toward that goal, even after all this time.

It's okay to not have it all figured out.

It's okay to be a work in progress.

how do i live in the in-between?

I can't tell you how many times I still feel like a middle school girl.

Something happens, and it's like I'm transported right back to 1991. It may be because I've raised some middle school girls in recent years. The things they encounter and struggle with feel oddly like the things 1991 Sarah encountered and struggled with: a changing body, feelings of insecurity, uncertainty about what life will look like next year.

In both stages of life, I've felt very much in the in-between.

Between jobs.

Between friends.

Between relationships.

Between interests.

Between jeans sizes.

I feel like I'm standing in a gap between what once was and what will be.

When my daughter started her period, she was essentially standing in that gap. She didn't want to stop being a kid, but she recognized that this very change defined her next season as a woman. She still likes to play with slime and is now only slightly grossed out at the idea of kissing a boy. In the words of the great Britney Spears, it feels like she's not a girl, not yet a woman.

She's in the in-between.

And now, in my forties, I feel the same way.

Truth be told, this isn't the first time I've found myself smack dab in the middle of the middle.

In 2006 my first book was published. I felt on top of the world. I was published in my twenties and was so proud to have built a career out of writing and speaking. In fact, I once got to travel all the way around the world to a tiny island in the South Pacific to speak. The same island was hosting the comedians James Avery (Uncle Phil from *The Fresh Prince of Bel-Air*) and Stephen Root (Milton from *Office Space*). I was rubbing elbows and eating dinner with celebrities! I felt like I ruled the world.

As most authors do, I also worked a day job to help support my creative endeavors. That job was as an editor for a nonprofit curriculum house. I feel lucky to have worked for a creative organization because it helped make me a better writer and communicator. Sure, I wasn't the shiniest star on the team, but the work I did felt like it was furthering my education.

Then everything changed.

Scott and I decided to move to be near family since we were growing our own family. At the time, Sinclair was two and I was pregnant with Rory. We made the decision with permission from the company I worked for. I could work remotely and still come back to town periodically for in-person events and meetings. This was well before 2020 thrust us into the working-remotely age, so having a full-time employee in another state was kind of a new concept at the time. After about six months of me working remotely, they made the decision that all employees needed to be local.

That decision pushed me smack-dab into the in-between. I could look behind and see what had been, but I had no idea what would be. I wish I could say it was just a few months of standing in that awkward space, but it wasn't. Months turned into years, and any hope of moving out of the in-between had faded. I wondered if I had peaked, if my career was over. Maybe I had too much success too early in life. Published author, global communicator, sought-after speaker, employed editor—it all just sort of ended.

Those years of in-between were dark. They were hard. I didn't feel like myself. I felt lost, without direction. I had worked for a decade toward something that seemed amazing.

Then it all changed.

Now what?

How do I live in the in-between?

That's the question that raced through my brain each night during that season of life. It's a question that often still keeps me awake at night. I think it's a question we all wonder in the in-between seasons of our lives.

Circumstances have a way of initiating the in-between. Sometimes they are positive, like a new job, or a new relationship, or the birth of a first child. But sometimes they're something harder. In my life, that something has often looked like loss. Loss of a job, loss of a relationship, or loss of something I held close.

This in-between is not for the faint of heart, but it is coming for us either way. Life happens, things change, and we're left standing in the middle trying to figure out where to go next.

So what do we do while we're in this phase?

If you find yourself in an in-between season of life, let me share a few ideas that might help you. These are things I've done or am doing that have been meaningful. It's not an exhaustive list. I'm sure you could add to it. But here is what has helped me find meaning in the in-between. Here's what helped me not give up in that stage.

Practice Introspection

Five years after being let go from my job, I launched my podcast, *Surviving Sarah*. Those were five long years. I worked other jobs during that time, but nothing felt like forward motion. It all felt like I was biding my time. Looking back, I see those in-between years were for introspection.

Years of journaling.

Years of reading about and researching what I was interested in.

Years of getting curious.

Years of looking for what would be next.

I read books and kept journals. I looked for inspiration around every corner. If you find yourself in the in-between, I'd encourage you to do the same. Buy a journal and some pens you love. In your journal, ask questions of yourself. Be honest. Create space to be curious about where you are and where you want to go. Then find some books (hopefully like this one you're reading now!) and dig into them. Mark them up. Highlight and underline. Make notes in the margins.

Journaling isn't the only path for introspection. Take a walk or do something else outside. Move your body. Take a shower and dry your hair. I know that last suggestion may sound silly, but it works for me. Something about the white noise of the water and the hair dryer allows my mind to wonder. Go see a movie or concert. Pick up a marker, pen, or paintbrush. Experiencing other creative works often has a way of inspiring introspection and ideas of your own.

I've found that this process of introspection builds hope. These seasons can feel dark, uncertain, and hopeless, but introspection allows hope to spring forward, one step at a time.

It took years of introspection before I had the idea for a podcast. Even when it initially came to me, I wasn't sure it would work. The podcast wasn't guaranteed to catapult me out of this in-between stage, but the idea inspired me, and the inspiration gave me enough hope to give it a shot—to pursue it and see what would happen.

Then it all changed—this time for the better!

It worked! The podcast grew. And I was writing again. After only a few years of podcasting, I signed a two-book contract with a major publishing house. I felt like maybe, finally, I'd made my way out of the in-between.

After the first book in the new publishing deal launched, I found myself in a place where I could look back at what was; I could see all I had accomplished. But the future? Well, it somehow still looked uncertain. When you work for yourself in a creative industry, you often find yourself back in the in-between. Projects end and other projects are waiting to begin. The plans I had for future work involving podcasts and books halted. I found myself looking back at what was and staring into the unknown of what was to come. This whole in-between thing was starting to feel like an episode of *Stranger Things*. Welcome back to the Upside Down.

Welcome back to the In-Between.

Feeling lost, uncertain, afraid. Wondering if I'd peaked. Lacking clarity. Questioning my identity and worth. I felt those things all over again. Again, I was left with a question.

How do I live in the in-between?

Back to introspection.

Back to journaling.

Back to reading.

Back to searching.

Back to getting curious.

As life would have it, my husband found himself in the in-between not too long ago. That place looked like working a job but also desiring to work on a passion project. When he is in that space, he feels uncertain.

My daughter is also in the in-between. She's in the throes of middle school feeling unsure of herself. Not liking how she looks, feeling uncertain about which activities she would enjoy, not knowing which friend group to hang out with. One night, as I put her to bed, she cried as I hugged her. She was hurt and confused and insecure. I made my way downstairs to find Scott in a similar state. I listened as he poured out his hurt, confusion, and frustration about his place in life. The in-between is hard for all of us.

Though their seasons of in-between were vastly different, I inadvertently gave them both the same advice: *It won't always be this way.*

I don't want that phrase to sound trite, so please don't read it that way. I say it sincerely because it has helped me. I say it because I need to remember it too.

My last in-between season lasted five years. Did it feel like a lifetime? Absolutely, yes, but it wasn't. Sure, it may be "this way" for a long time, but no matter how long, it won't always be this way. Life is always moving, changing, and evolving. So, then, are we.

One night recently, when Scott was out of town for work, I found myself just wanting to sit in my feelings. The girls had gone to bed, so I poured a glass of wine, crawled under my covers, and watched *Hope Floats*. Gosh, I love that movie. Let me tell you, that movie hits different watching it as a middle-aged woman than it does watching it as a teenager. Sure, Harry Connick Jr. is still charming, but the grief in that movie is nearly palpable to me now. As the movie closed, I kept thinking about how applicable it was to the in-between. Sandra Bullock's character narrates to us the truth about change as she says,

> Beginnings are scary, endings are usually sad, but it is the middle that counts the most. You need to remember that when you find yourself at the beginning. Just give hope a chance to float up.[3]

I just sat and sobbed into my glass of wine at the truth of her words.

I'm in the middle. Scott is in the middle. My daughter is in the middle. You're likely in the middle too.

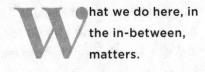

What we do here, in the in-between, matters.

What we do here, in the in-between, matters. So we just have to keep looking, keep being curious, keep moving forward.

We have to give hope a chance to float up. Introspection is like forward motion. It reminds us to keep paying attention. It allows our hearts and minds to be on alert, watching for hope to bubble up.

Say Yes

If you're reading this book, then you've lived long enough to know that change is inevitable. Change is practically around the corner for each of us. I don't think I paid much attention to that reality when I was younger. As an adult, however, I see the fallout of change all the time. And change often feels like loss.

Loss of a job.

Loss of being in a physical location for our jobs.

Loss of loved ones.

Loss of health.

Loss of traditions.

Loss of what was normal.

The year we moved brought a change in location for many others as well. We moved from our cozy, tight-knit community outside of Atlanta back to my hometown in Tennessee. Another close friend left her hometown for the middle of nowhere. Another friend left her childhood hometown to move to a whole new state. Each of us was starting something new and feeling uncertain.

I recently asked one of those friends about how her family adjusted to the move. She replied that the move was hard and she spent a few months grumbling about it. But eventually, she decided she needed to accept her new reality. Could I do that? Could I accept my new reality when that reality felt like an in-between? Keep in mind, I'd recently googled "How do you accept the things you cannot change?" Clearly, I'm looking for answers related to change.

I asked her what acceptance looked like for her. On one hand, her answer surprised me, and on the other, it didn't. She said, "I just started saying yes to everything."

Yes to this neighborhood.

Yes to this church.

Yes to this school.

Yes to this job.

Yes to carpooling and driving tweens to school. (That deserves a badge of honor!)

Yes to hosting neighbors for dinner.

Yes, yes, yes.

Over time, acceptance followed, but it started with a simple yes.

Her response had me wondering about my struggle with acceptance. Could saying yes be the answer? Does most of my angst come from my resistance to saying yes? My insistence on saying no? Is that how I've become my own worst enemy in the in-between?

One of the biggest changes I fight is aging. Maybe most

of us resist aging. When I turned forty, I remember being unsettled. In fact, I had a total toddler tantrum about it. I looked at Scott and said, "I might as well be sixty! That is literally around the corner." Scott kindly reminded me how much life I'd lived between twenty and forty, which means there's a lot of life to live between forty and sixty. I guess he's right.

Aging is out of my control. It's a change that's coming whether I accept it or not.

Since Google didn't have the answer I was looking for, I decided to take my friend's words to heart.

I just said yes to everything.

You're two sizes bigger? Yes.

Your face isn't as youthful? Yes.

You're in your midforties? Yes.

When it comes to aging, saying yes doesn't mean throwing in the towel. I need to take care of myself. It's good to strength train. It's good to care about what I eat. It's good to wash my face. Acceptance doesn't change that, but it does stop the resistance. The resistance is what drives the voice in my head that's always saying there's more to do or that what I'm doing isn't enough. The resistance makes me feel like I don't have as much worth as a middle-aged woman. The resistance makes me work so hard to fight the extra weight or the wrinkles around my eyes. It's self-protection. Self-protection from feeling vulnerable to whatever may cause unacceptance.

Saying yes doesn't apply only to aging. There are plenty of ways we feel vulnerable in this season of life—plenty of things that cause us to want to self-protect. Saying yes is the antidote to resistance. That simple response has the potential to unlock so much happiness. When you say yes to the book club or yes to lunch or yes to the neighborhood gathering, you are fighting the resistance. You are fighting the urge to self-protect.

So what if the response needed as we change looks less like resistance and more like an invitation? Acceptance is an invitation. It's an invitation to acknowledge where you are and who you are. It's an invitation to allow someone to love you for who you are. It's an invitation to stand in the vulnerability instead of resisting it.

It's an invitation to say yes.

Be Open to Therapy

Saying yes isn't easy. In fact, just as I wrote this portion of the chapter, I shut my computer feeling pretty good. So good that I decided to get dressed even though I had nowhere to go. I took off my current uniform—workout leggings—and put on jeans and a new sweater. I even went so far as to curl my dirty hair.

Where should I go? Well, like anyone who spends their days with a flexible schedule does, I went to the grocery store. (When did going to Publix turn into an outing? This may be part of aging too, huh?)

I walked into Publix feeling good about myself. I felt good about being vulnerable with you. I felt good about being okay with who I am and where I am. I felt good about saying yes and accepting my jeans size.

For all of about four minutes. And then I didn't feel that way anymore. That cool acceptance was gone. I literally walked the aisles of Publix saying, "You're okay," over and over to myself, trying to coach myself that the jeans size is okay, my body is okay. By the time I pulled the car up to my house, I'd said on repeat to myself the exact things I said to you about acceptance.

Say yes to the jeans size.

Don't resist; accept.

It's an invitation.

I'll be honest. It didn't work in the moment.

That's why this season is hard. It's not like you see the problem, hear a potential solution, and then—boom—it's all resolved. It's not one time in the ring with acceptance and you never struggle again. It just doesn't work that way.

I'm still me.

I'm still human.

I'm still a work in progress.

In the words of another great pop princess, Taylor Swift, "It's me. Hi. I'm the problem, it's me."

As I sat in the car, I was reminded of something else that helps me in the in-between: therapy.

Like I said, aging hasn't been easy. I have resisted it. I have feared it. I want to always look the way I did at twenty-seven, but I'm now forty-four. I've bought too many lies sold by magazines and social media that tell me that looking like I'm in my twenties should be possible. I've seen enough celebrities and influencers to convince myself that it is possible. That's why saying yes is really hard in this area of in-between. And ultimately, that's why I decided to go to therapy.

I'm tired of resisting and finding myself right back in the same cycle.

Maybe you are too. You may not be struggling with your body changing, but something else has probably left you standing in the in-between. Maybe you struggle with work or your sense of happiness in relationships. Maybe you feel like you're in the in-between with friendships or even faith. One of the best things I've found to help me stop resisting and work on acceptance is talking with someone trained to help me find a better way. I believe the same can be true for you.

Sometimes we need more than what a friend or a book can offer. I know therapy is a privilege. It can be expensive, and sometimes hard choices have to be made and there just isn't enough time or money for therapy. I can only afford to go once a month, so I save up all my stories and struggles until I can unleash them. Even a couple of sessions could be a helpful start. Or maybe your church offers counseling at a discounted price. Or maybe you could sit and talk with someone older and wiser from time to time. No matter what's available to you, if you find yourself in the in-between and it is overwhelming, talk therapy can be a useful tool to guide you forward.

Grieve

Acceptance is not an easy task. One of the most important things I've done to help myself accept my status in the in-between and be able to move on is to grieve. If I want to be open to what could be, I have to grieve what was, what is, or what didn't happen.

I am a driven, competitive person. I love having a clear vision of where to go and a plan to get there. I work hard and love the process. That's exactly what I loved about diving in to start my podcast. But after building the podcast and seeing great success, I noticed some changes. In the first couple of years, the show had grown exponentially. Podcasts were relatively new then, so more and more people were discovering them for the first time. By 2018 podcasts were growing not only in listeners but in the number of available shows. More people were launching their own show every day. By 2020 Apple Podcasts had one million shows, a number that doubled in 2021. And now in 2023? There are an estimated three to four million shows.

During my months of introspection, I thought about where I saw myself down the road. I thought about whether the podcast was still worth continuing. Ultimately, I realized that the podcast wasn't going to achieve what I was striving toward.

Looking back with pride at what I had accomplished while also looking forward and knowing it wouldn't be what I really wanted it to be felt a lot like grief. I had worked so hard and built the podcast all by myself. I was a one-woman show. I did everything, from the administration of bookings, to research and conversation curation, to editing, promotion, design, and execution. It was a lot, and I was tired. But making a change brought grief because endings are sad, even when you know it's the right call.

Part of what I was grieving was the loss of what could

have been and what didn't happen. Sitting with the pain of what didn't happen is hard. I've felt grief around job opportunities that didn't come to fruition. I've felt grief around relationships that never had a chance to grow. I've felt grief because of bad timing. Part of living in a season of in-between is allowing ourselves to feel the grief.

I'm no expert in dealing with grief. And I continue to discover more work I need to do in this area. But if grief is a common emotion that we experience during the in-between times, I have to learn to deal with it. So that's what I'm trying to do. I'm learning to look fondly on what was, allow myself to feel sad for what is, and at the same time, hold space for what could be.

I'm learning to look fondly on what was, allow myself to feel sad for what is, and at the same time, hold space for what could be.

Shift Your Perspective

In the years before I started the podcast, my girls were little. Sadly, I found it hard to be present with them then because I always had my eyes on the horizon, watching for what was next. It's good to be hopeful and watchful. It's good to dream and think about all the possibilities. But like all good things, too much is too much. Focusing on the future sometimes meant I missed out on the present.

Unfortunately, it's a mistake I've made more than once.

I was reminded of this lesson recently after having

coffee with a friend. We hadn't seen each other in over a year. Of course, we had seen each other's lives displayed online, but, as I know and you know, that isn't always what's happening in the nitty-gritty of our actual lives. As we talked, she opened up about what her year had really been like. She'd faced so many hard things tucked into one year. She was walking through relationship loss, extraordinarily hard days with her teenage child, and complicated health issues.

In summary, for her, when it rained, it really did pour.

As I drove home and processed all that she told me, I was reminded of the angst I had been feeling. Her life helped put my life in perspective. Now, I do believe that whatever we find hard in our own lives doesn't need to be compared with what's hard in someone else's. We don't have to shame ourselves for carrying something "less difficult." But sometimes shifting our perspective helps. As I felt lost, sad, and angsty about my in-between, I remembered what she was carrying, not to compare but to change my perspective, to see my circumstances for what they were: hard, yes, but not unbearable.

I wrote a whole chapter about gratitude in *A Mother's Guide to Raising Herself*. I talked about asking my girls, "What made you smile?" as a way to help them notice the good in their days. Gratitude helps us notice what's good right now, today, in the present tense. It's easy to let this practice fall by the wayside when I'm in the in-between. If I let you look through my journal, you'd see only a handful of days over the last year where I talked about what I was thankful for. I was lacking perspective, thinking too much about the future and too much about the past. I wasn't sitting in the present and looking around to remember what was good.

When we find ourselves in the in-between, practicing gratitude is vital. To make ourselves look up and out at what is right now. To see the good around us.

So make your list. Shift your perspective. Look for the good. I did exactly that today as I finished writing.

I'm thankful for . . .

My home
Big windows to see the yard
Horses grazing
Iced coffee on my desk

Gratitude is needed more than ever when we find ourselves in the in-between.

It has the power to move us forward.

It has the power to provide perspective.

It has the power to help us not just see the good but experience it every step of the way.

Whether or not you find yourself in a season of in-between right now, you are guaranteed to find yourself there at some point. Life has a way of landing us smack-dab back in a place of asking that question:

How do I live in the in-between?

We can't run from it, hide from it, or buy our way out of it. We have to live in it for as long as it lasts. That doesn't mean life can't be enjoyed in the middle of it. Find what works for you. Dig deep into introspection and find

someone who can help you navigate your complicated feelings during this time. And then look up and notice the good
around you in this season. Find what helps you to cultivate
a sense of peace and happiness in the murky in-between.
And stay curious, because one day you'll look up and realize
you are out of that season and fully emerged in what was
to come.

does anyone like me?

17,375.

It seems a little odd to start a chapter with a number. I mean, this is a book, not a math problem. If I promise not to make you do any long division, or ask you to figure out the square root of anything, or force any other math-like activity on you, will you just go with me here?

This number represents all the people I'm connected to online. People from Instagram, Facebook, Pinterest, my podcast *Surviving Sarah*, and my newsletter. At first glance, you might think, "Man, that's a lot of 'friends.'" You might even suspect that if someone has that many "friends" online, they probably feel pretty connected to people, both in their online world and in their everyday life. After all, someone struggling to connect with others couldn't possibly build an online audience of more than seventeen thousand people, right?

One could assume that, yes, but you and I both know that's not true. We know that just because you're connected to that many people online doesn't necessarily mean you feel connected to even one person in real life.

We know that because we've probably experienced it.

We live in such a strange time. We have access to everything and everyone. And that access is instant. If we have a question, we go right to Google for an instant answer. If we want to share an opinion, we post it on Twitter or

Facebook for an instant response. If we want to tell people about our cool vacations, latest accomplishments, or family successes, we share them on Instagram for instant applause. More than ever before, connection is literally at our fingertips.

Then why are we so lonely?

Even though we are "connected" more than ever before, loneliness is through the roof. A survey in 2019 showed that 58 percent of Americans felt like no one in their life knew them well.[4] In a survey in 2021, Americans reported fewer close friendships than ever.[5] Even though 17,375 people have access to me online, I don't feel seen. I don't feel known. I don't feel connected. I don't know if people like me. Instead of me staying awake at night thinking about all my "friends," I have this pressing question running through my brain in the wee hours:

Does anyone like me?

In the dark of night, you may ask yourself the same.

In my life, loneliness has come in waves and seasons.

Motherhood definitely brought lessons in loneliness. When my girls were babies, life felt like the movie *Groundhog Day*. Every day felt the same. I didn't go out much simply because doing so felt like running a marathon. I had to remember 1,200 items just to get out the door: diapers, wipes, extra clothes, socks, pacifiers, snacks, bottles, and creams. My designer diaper bag likely weighed fifty pounds. No wonder I had back issues during those years! Because going out was such a hassle, those years were lonely. Tucked inside our home, waiting for each hour to click over to the next one, I wondered if I'd ever feel any less alone as a parent.

Then came the middle years of parenting, which were exponentially less lonely. There were playdates to be had, classes to join, and activities to try. The comradery picked up its pace. I could just lock eyes with another mom at Target in a similar stage of life and feel connected. With one glance, I knew she knew me. She knew my pain. She knew my exhaustion. She knew my relief at coming out of those early, lonely years. Talking to other moms about the hardship of these years was easy. Whether it was tackling potty training, handling tantrums, or figuring out third-grade math, we were in it together. We assured ourselves that everything we were dealing with in that season was simply developmental. One day our kids would figure out how to go to the bathroom. They would likely stop throwing fits in public places. Eventually they'd figure out multiplication.

Looking back, those elementary years were pretty golden. Friendships were just waiting to bloom, and I flourished in them when they did.

But now that I'm squarely in the teen years, loneliness has settled in once again. Gone are the days of locking eyes with another mother and feeling the kinship between us. Mothers at this age rarely see the outside of their cars. We're hardly ever in a place to make eye contact with another mother. There are no more school class parties or fall festivals for us to attend. Kids hop on the bus after school or into a parked car. The closest we get to interacting with other parents is through sports. But even then, it can be hard to truly connect. Rory joined the tennis team in seventh grade along with six other girls. The problem? Those six girls have all known each other forever. Rory was the lone outsider; so was her mother. Breaking into the group of parents was just as hard for me as breaking into the group of girls was for Rory.

While proximity is a factor in our loneliness, the biggest hindrance to connecting with other parents at this stage might be fear. We are afraid to open up about what's going on with our teenagers because we don't know what we'll find on the other side of our confession. The things we deal with in this stage of parenting feel heavier than whether my kid was potty trained by the age of three. Sharing these struggles is harder than confiding in another mother about toddler meltdowns. The judgment feels stronger. If a teen chooses to vape, create provocative TikToks, or sext, it is seen as a reflection on the parent.

It's no wonder parents of teens are scared to open up! Vulnerability is always scary because opening ourselves up—letting ourselves be seen—involves risk. We risk being rejected. We risk being judged. We risk being uninvited. We risk not being liked. We risk becoming an outcast.

As I mentioned earlier, I launched my blog and podcast when the girls were toddlers. I documented what we ate, sharing our gluten-free and dairy-free meal plans. I shared fashion ideas and home ideas. And I shared what I was learning about raising kids. My motivation has always been to connect and relate to others, so on those early podcast episodes, I shared openly about my life—and my kids' lives. I remember my mentor, Kellee, cautioning me one day to be careful about what I shared. She reminded me that one day, my kids will be able to listen to every single episode and read every post. My kids could barely read books beyond Dr. Seuss at that point, so her advice felt crazy, but I knew she was right. I listened to her advice and worked on not oversharing. I worked on not sharing negative things. I worked on being vague about which kid was doing what. I definitely didn't do it well all the time, but I tried.

Maybe your experience with loneliness has nothing to do with motherhood. Loneliness comes in all shapes and sizes. For you, it may be more about work. If that's the case, then just know I feel that too. The pandemic of 2020 turned everything upside down, and it for sure changed the landscape of work. Buildings used to be filled with people who could connect in the kitchen while pouring another cup of coffee. We could connect as we sat together in a meeting, laughing with our eyes over an inside joke. Or we could connect by grabbing a spontaneous lunch together. We had daily social interactions like that.

Now many jobs have moved remote. And no matter how often you see people on a Zoom call, it doesn't provide the same feeling of connection that in-person work does. It's just not the same. I'd started to feel the weight of the loneliness of my work before 2020, but the sheer emotional exhaustion of that time was a like a giant highlighter to my isolation. Working from home, for myself and by myself, suddenly wasn't as ideal.

Recently, I read an article in the *Harvard Business Review* about exhaustion and work. In it, the authors described how I was feeling about work at the time. They made the point that there is a significant correlation between feelings of loneliness and work exhaustion. They said that the more exhausted people become, the lonelier they feel.[6] I stared at that statement and read it again. This was exactly my problem. Everything about the work I was doing involved me, myself, and I. Yes, I had to shoulder every task. Yes, I felt exhausted at times. But the real exhaustion came from being so isolated—having no one to work with. The job itself didn't exhaust me, the isolation of it did.

I'm sure I could ask every single one of you reading this book right now what kind of isolation is currently exhausting you. Maybe it's not your kids or your job. Maybe it's your relationship, or an illness, or a move to a new city. The cause may be different for each of us, but the effect is the same. At this stage in life, when we are knee-deep in raising kids, maybe over a decade into a relationship with a significant other, and decades into our career, we are ripe for loneliness.

So what do we do about it? How do we push past the fear of connecting? How do we take the risk of opening up and being known? How do we not feel so lonely?

I'm going to share with you what I've learned. It's not rocket science. They probably aren't going to ask me to give a TED Talk about any of it. I share simply what has helped me to feel less lonely in this season.

Reach Out

First, reach out. I bet you wish I didn't just say that. Trust me, I don't like the suggestion either. I would much rather have someone reach out to me. I want to receive an invitation to a gathering. I want to be asked to go for a walk. I want to be included in dinner plans. I don't want to be the one to reach out. But if you want to be less lonely, sometimes you have to take matters into your own hands. Sometimes you have to be the one to reach out.

> **If you want to be less lonely, sometimes you have to take matters into your own hands. Sometimes you have to be the one to reach out.**

I recently shared a meme on Instagram that basically said, at this point in the winter season, I've hit the point where once I get back home, I'm not going back out. Staying home is just easier than going out. But what if that mentality has contributed to our loneliness?

I'm writing this chapter in the midst of the holiday season, and nearly every gift guide I've seen has included an idea for the friend who stays home. Yes, we now celebrate and encourage each other just to tuck in at home. Don't get me wrong. I'm not suggesting you go clubbing every night. I'm pretty sure my fortysomething-year-old body wouldn't be able to handle such a thing. If they played "Get Low" by Lil Jon, I may never be able to get back up off the floor! All I'm saying is that we need to stop glorifying staying home.

The shutdown in 2020 did a number on us. We were forced to stay inside for so long that we forgot how to live outside our four walls. Friendships have always been hard, but I think they took on an extra hurdle after that. Our worlds grew so small in that season that most people saw only those who lived in their house or right next door. Most interactions were online instead of in person. Everything from shopping to meals to movies to the gym to church moved from in-person with others to online at home. Yet here we are, years later, sometimes still living like we are in a shutdown. I think we've grown used to staying in. But we can't get so used to our comfort zone at home that we miss all that's waiting for us if we initiate relationships and in-person connection. We need to put ourselves out there again!

Listen, I know all the reasons and all the excuses running through your head.

I know you're tired.
I know you're an introvert.
I know you don't actually like people.
I know it's raining.
I know it's cold.
I know showing up might feel awkward.

Can I be honest with you for a second?

You're not too tired.
You're not too shy.
You're not too busy.
The weather will change.
It might be awkward, but it also might be great.

I know because I've had to fight off these same excuses in my effort to find friendships in this season.

Has it been hard? Yes! But has it been worth it? Most of the time, yes. Establishing friendships and building connections are crucial to your happiness. We were made for community—it's hardwired into us. We have it in us to build connections, but we have to make the effort to put ourselves out there to find them.

One of my closest friends moved back to Tennessee at the same time that I did. We lamented over the reality that finding friends was harder at this stage. As we talked about it, she eventually came up with an idea. Most of our conversations with each other were about books. (No one told me that midlife would turn me into a book nerd, but I'm here for it!) She said there had to be more people like us in this town—people longing for connection who had a common love for books. Her way of reaching out to find friends? Starting a book club. Nearly forty people showed up for the first club meeting! Clearly, she was right.

People wanted to get out.

People wanted to be invited.

People wanted connection.

And people like books.

You don't have to start a book club (but maybe you should!). Figure out something unique to you. Invite someone to walk weekly or to meet up for coffee. You may not hit it off, but that's okay. Making the effort to reach out is a step in the right direction.

Reaching out doesn't have to be a big, bold move. What if you simply texted a friend every day? Or even shot them an email? Or took advantage of apps like Voxer and Marco Polo to connect regularly with someone? Start with a small gesture—a small act of reaching out. And then build on it.

I spent years building a friendship with someone when I lived in Atlanta. We were on a group text that texted fairly often, but it wasn't until COVID-19 hit that we started really developing our friendship. Because the world was shut down, we decided to take walks together every Friday morning. We could maintain social distance easily, and walks were a much-needed escape from our houses. Our walks were long strolls through the downtown neighborhoods in which we lived. Some mornings we were gone for over two hours. When we both moved away at the end of 2020, you know what happened? Our friendship continued to grow. Instead of walking in person on Friday mornings, we took virtual walks together at the same time. Every Friday, we called each other and talked. We still do that even now, all these years later. What started as small, consistent text messages led to daily, in-person time. Our friendship has been built over time, but it started with one small step to reach out.

I recently heard about a study by a University of Kansas professor who discovered the actual amount of time it takes to develop a friendship. "He estimated it takes between forty and sixty hours to form a casual friendship, eighty to one hundred hours to transition to being a friend and more than two hundred hours together to become good friends."[7] That's a lot of time! No wonder we have a hard time building friendships in this season of life! We may feel that our lives are already busy. And we live in a culture that wants instant everything. But friendships develop over time. A lot of time.

Seeing and Being Seen

We all have a hardwired desire to be seen. That's part of being a social creature. Being seen requires us also to see other people. Doing this may look like finding friends in unexpected places. I started working out at a local studio in 2021. Talk about moving past vulnerability! Showing up to work out is vulnerable. You don't know what you're doing. You risk looking stupid, not to mention weak. You may not have the right stylish workout clothes. Seriously, my first day there everyone was wearing styled outfits by lululemon, and I showed up in yoga pants from T.J.Maxx and a ratty T-shirt. I felt intimidated, but I stuck it out because I knew I not only needed the exercise but also needed to be around people. The friendships I developed by showing up weekly to that studio were a pleasant surprise. They were unexpected. These friends range in age from twenty-five to seventy-five. Our common ground is the studio. That was all we needed to develop a friendship. We just had to be willing to be present and then look outside ourselves to see each other.

When it comes to "seeing" others, we also need to be willing to look outside the box. I've become unexpected friends with my seventy-six-year-old neighbor. Would I normally look for friendship with people nearly three decades older than I am? Probably not. But our proximity encouraged me to reach out to her. And I'm so glad I opened my eyes to see her! We built a friendship on the common ground of horses. She has been a wealth of knowledge, help, and guidance, and I would have missed out on her friendship if I hadn't initiated a conversation.

Maybe the same could be true for you! Start by looking around. Who could you reach out to? A neighbor? A parent on your kid's team? Your kid's teacher? Someone from work? Simply let proximity help you find someone unexpected. Then look at a current need or interest. If you need to work out, let the greater need of connection be the motivation to make it to the gym. Join the book club (or start it!). Maybe even reach out to volunteer or work somewhere. Then invite others to join you. Put yourself in places to find the friends you want in this season of life.

I sat with my middle schooler at a recent tennis match. I mentioned earlier that she's new to the team and the rest of the girls have played on teams together their whole lives. It's been hard for her to break into that group of friends. Three of the girls were sitting together watching something on a phone. Rory stood up to go join them, but she had to sort of sit behind them. I'm not sure these girls even knew she was there. I watched as she was not included. To be clear, it wasn't on purpose. These girls weren't trying to be exclusive. They just were. She sat on the outside edge of the group for a few minutes, waiting to be noticed, before she finally came back to sit with me.

My heart ached. I knew exactly how she felt. Over the years, I've been in her shoes more times than I can count. I told her that it sucks not to be seen. It hurts. I told her that not many people know what it's like to be the new kid on the block. I, too, moved to a new city when I was ten years old. I remember what it was like to step into a world of established friendships right at the awkward stage of middle school. Unfortunately, I know it in my current season of life too.

I told her that as hard as that was, it allowed me to become someone who sees others. I told her that because of what I experienced, I have always seen the people who aren't seen. It's sort of like a superpower. I can walk into a room and notice the person who needs to be noticed. I do that because I have been that person. I think that's what drew me to work in ministry as a young adult. I wanted to make sure that people felt seen, noticed.

Be the person who sees people. And then be brave. Seeing people and reaching out and extending invitations all require courage. People may say no. They may not reciprocate interest. And that's scary. Doing scary things requires courage. But to move out of the loneliness, we have to be willing to take the step, take the initiative, and extend the invitation.

Live Your Life Assuming People Like You

One of the biggest lies we believe about ourselves that limits our ability to reach out or even accept an invitation is this:

I don't think people like me.

Yes, this is one of those beliefs that burns through my mind at 3:00 a.m. when I'm wide awake with anxiety. I play back the day in detail, collecting evidence as to why I think nobody likes me. Maybe I wasn't invited to something. Maybe someone never responded to my text. Maybe someone gave me a strange look. To me, it all adds up to one thing: nobody likes me. And as long as I believe that, I will always be on the lookout for ways to confirm that it must be true.

The core of that belief, that tension, speaks to what I think about myself. Do I believe I am worth liking? And I can take it a step further and ask, Do I even like myself?

The struggle starts there—with me. And I think it starts there for you too. Many of us, if we're honest, don't really like ourselves. We don't see what others like about us. That's because we are our own worst critic. We struggle to list good qualities about ourselves but run out of paper when listing the negative ones. It's no wonder we're afraid that no one likes us.

How do I get rid of that fear? How do I learn to like myself so that I can overcome the limiting belief that nobody else likes me? How do I keep this fear of not being liked from limiting my ability to be known? How do I keep it from limiting my ability to be seen and to build connection?

I think it starts with noticing the good in myself.

I recently sat in my therapist's office unpacking something along a similar vein. She asked me if there was anything I liked about my body. I have to admit it took me a while to answer. I finally answered that I usually like my hair and sometimes my face. That's a start. First, I need to focus on what I like about myself.

So I ask you the same: What do you like about you?

Maybe you like your personality or the way you laugh. Maybe you like that you are punctual or always dependable. Maybe you like that you are someone who remembers details about someone's life. We need to start noticing the good things about ourselves because those are the things that others like too. We need to let those things—those attributes and qualities—speak for themselves so we can believe that, deep down at the core of who we are, we are likable.

My oldest always assumes that people don't like her. I can't tell you how many times she's told me that so-and-so doesn't like her, but every time I see my daughter around other people, it seems like the opposite is true. One instance stands out in my mind. In middle school, my daughter told me about a girl who clearly didn't like her. I asked her how she knew, and she didn't have any real evidence. She just knew it to be true. Fast-forward to the next year, and I heard her talking about this same girl. I wondered out loud, "Didn't you say that she didn't like you?" Her response? "No! She's great! Turns out she's always liked me." My daughter just *assumed* this person didn't like her. She made up an entire story in her head to affirm that belief, but it wasn't true. What difference would it make in your life if you believed that people like you and that you are likable? Finding connection might be slightly easier if we held that belief.

I'd be wrong not to leave you with this disclaimer: not everybody will like you. That's a tough pill for me to swallow. Most of us want everyone to like us. But we are all wired differently and connect with different people in different ways. So it's okay if not everyone likes you. If you have one or two friends you can call or text when you really need someone, then you're good.

The loneliness we feel is real. And it's far too easy to stay in it instead of working to find our way into the lives of others. It's easy to live closed off and not allow ourselves to be seen. It's simpler not to reach out if there's a chance of rejection. But I've seen firsthand that connection to others really does make the world go round. We need each other. We need to have some people in our real life whom we can call.

If you feel lonely and are wondering if you're likable, know that you most certainly are likable. Then reach out to someone. Reach out again. And probably again. You don't have to have 17,375 friends. You only need one. Look around. Look in unexpected places. And find some common ground to build connection.

will my family be okay?

Do you ever think back to the days of your youth? Before you related to all the memes about the fact that adulting is hard? Before you had to be the one responsible for paying all the bills? Before you had to make sure that other people had what they needed to survive the day? I've tried to think back to those days—to the days when I was still young enough that my responsibility and stress in life were very low. I remember my sweet, twentysomething self. She was bright eyed—because she was so well rested (I don't remember struggling with sleep in my twenties)—and pretty naive about what it takes to care for people more than just yourself.

For me, sleeplessness didn't enter the scene until Sinclair was born. They tell you that having a baby will bring on some sleepless nights. They just don't tell you that the sleepless nights will last for the rest of your life!

When my kids were young, I would lie awake nervous that they wouldn't sleep through the night. I would wonder if I heard something. Was that a cry? Was that a door opening? Was that a voice? A stomach bug is going around; is tonight our night to be taken down?

As the girls have aged, that same sleepless worry has remained. Only now I'm worrying about so much more than a baby's cry or a stomach bug (truth be told, I still worry about the stomach bug). Now I worry about their future. I worry about their friendships. I worry about our relationship.

Making decisions about life is a lot easier when you're the only one who will be affected. When I decided to move across the country when I was twenty-two years old, it wasn't as difficult as it would be to make that decision now. If needed, I could adjust sails pretty easily when I was on my own. But making decisions about change now with a husband and two kids is much harder.

I thought we would live in Atlanta for the rest of our lives or at least until our girls graduated high school. Sure, I fantasized about moving to the beach and having an ocean view (I still dream about that). But we loved where we lived. Our girls grew up in that small town just north of Atlanta. We built a good life. My girls both had friends—friends they'd grown up with since the ages of three and five. They had imagined their future there.

But Scott and I both had something inside us that pointed us in a different direction. We had felt unsettled for a couple of years. Every year, when our rental lease was up for renewal, we entertained the idea of moving. We reevaluated where we were in life and where we wanted to be in the future. And each year, we had always landed on remaining where we were. Until 2020.

Deciding to leave the area where our girls called home to move to another state wasn't easy. We ended up making it quickly, but just because it was quick didn't mean it was easy. I spent countless nights lying awake worrying about the move. The weight of it felt like sleeping under a weighted blanket. It was heavy on my heart. I could manage my fears about how the move would impact me, but managing the ones about how this move would impact the girls? That felt nearly impossible.

What if they don't make any friends?

What if they don't find a place to belong?

What if they're miserable?

What if they get homesick?

Will they hate us for making them leave a place and people they loved?

That last question is a real one. The first few I could deal with, but the last one? The one about the very real relationship and connection I have with my daughters? That is the one that kept me tossing and turning all night. The real worry underneath it all was the fear of losing connection— fear of losing the relationship with my daughters. At the end of the day, I was worried about my family and the repercussions that would come with this change.

Will my family be okay?

Of course, this question extends beyond those of us with kids. We care and worry about our partner, our parents, all our family members. At the root of our worry, I think this is the question we're truly contemplating.

If I move to a new city,

If I send them to a different school,

If I go back to work,

If my marriage ends,

If illness comes,

If the unthinkable comes knocking on my door . . .
Will my family be okay?

A friend of mine said she worries about how long she will live—how much of her kids' lives she will be able to see. If it's not as much as she hopes, will they be okay?

Sure, some of our worries as parents may be far-fetched, but I think most of them are grounded in reality. The stakes of life feel higher at this stage. We've seen enough to know life doesn't always go the way we hope, and we want to do whatever we can to make sure our kids will be okay.

And at the end of the day, we just want to know that our family will be okay. That no matter what happens or doesn't, they will be okay.

Fear is at the root of that question: Will my family be okay? Sometimes that fear or worry comes from the pressure to be all and do all. I understand that pressure. From the moment our children are born, we worry about their future. And depending on where you live, you may feel pressure about their future as early as preschool. I've met parents who based their preschool choice on where they hoped the child would go to college! I get it. We all want our kids to excel. We want them to be noticed. We want them to succeed. So we do more.

Rory has a friend involved in three sports and show choir in the seventh grade. And that's just one kid in the family! These families have multiple kids, and each kid does multiple activities. That's a lot of time and money. I wonder if that busyness is born out of this same worry about their future. We worry they won't be accepted in college without enough extracurriculars, so we sign them up for more programs. We worry they are missing out on fun and opportunities, so we encourage them to take on new activities. We worry they won't find their niche, so we push them into everything we can think of to help them figure it out. Why? Because we sincerely want them to have it all.

For better or for worse, our family decided early in our kids' lives to limit activities. That decision was made with my and Scott's best interests in mind as well as theirs. We only have so much time and money. We just can't do it all. Every yes means a no to something else. Sure, I disappoint my kids when I have to say no, but isn't that how the world works? We can't keep losing sleep because we're worried that our kids are missing out. We can't succumb to the pressure to be all and do all. It's not good for us, and it's not good for them.

Other times, shame is what keeps us awake at night. Parenting is a shame and judgment minefield. That's because none of us know what we are doing! There's no owner's manual. There's no guidebook for dummies on how to raise healthy, smart kids who still want to be in relationship with you when they're older. Sure, people claim to have the answers, but do they really? There are no guarantees in parenting. We are all wading through uncertainty and self-doubt. This is all a big trial-and-error experience.

I recently saw a meme that said, "My son just got a face tattoo, and he was breastfed. Go ahead and give the formula. It doesn't really matter what you do." Don't you wish you had heard that message when your kids were babies? We all want to believe there is one right way to parent, and if we can just find it, then our kids will be happy, healthy people.

Take technology, for example. There's no guidebook to tell us what to do. Every parent has a different approach. We know parents who gave their kids phones before age ten. We know parents who have allowed their kids on some form of social media as early as seven. And we know parents who didn't give their kids phones until they were in high school. There are a million opinions about the subject. We are just now starting to see some solid data around technology and kids. But until we have more data, we are all just trying to figure it out.

Or think about kids and sex. This is another topic that carries a lot of opinions. Some parents choose never to talk about the subject with their kids. Some parents choose to have one big conversation about it when they are older. And some parents choose to have conversations all along and start when they are young. So many opinions. So many emotions tied to those opinions. That is a shame minefield if I've ever seen one.

There are endless things to worry about when it comes to our kids and their future.

If she gets Snapchat, will she be okay?

If she receives a nude, will she be okay?

If she has sex, will she be okay?

So many things to worry about. And the shame part? We worry that what they do reflects on us.

If she gets Snapchat in middle school, what does that say about me?

If she receives a nude, what does that say about me?

If she has sex, what does that say about me?

Shame. We feel it in our chests and in our faces. My

heart rate races just thinking about it. What if I do something or allow something and judgment from others follows?

So we worry and worry and worry about what's to come. Or we worry and worry and worry about the shame we feel in failing. Either way, we're stuck. Either way, we risk a loss of connection with our kids. Either way, we lose sleep.

There has to be a better way, right?

I also lie awake at night and worry about Scott. Will he be okay? Will the stress he carries be too much? What can I do to alleviate his stress? Will our marriage withstand the years? If you are in a long-term relationship, I think you know what I'm describing. The underlying worry is the same as what I worry about with my kids: a loss of connection. I don't want Scott and I to lose connection as we grow, age, and evolve.

So if we can't be perfect—we'll inevitably do something that causes a fracture in connection—then what do we do? How do we build connection in these relationships for now and hopefully later?

Relationships Are Not To-Do Lists

There are two kinds of people: those who like people and those who don't. Typically, those two types of people find each other and get married. That's true for me and Scott. I'll let you guess which one of us is which.

We recently listed and sold our hay ring—a giant metal circle that holds big round bales of hay—on Facebook

Marketplace. Scott listed the item and told me that some cowboy-sounding man would be showing up to buy it. As the "cowboy" arrived at the house, we began a conversation—Scott, the cowboy, and I. We quickly established common ground: horses. He had twenty acres and seven horses, and that common ground kept us talking and talking. When he finally left, Scott was so relieved.

"I kept waiting for him to end the conversation," he told me. "If the roles were reversed, I would just want to buy the item and get out of there. But he genuinely seemed to just want to talk to us about horses. And you were the same."

This happens to us all the time. We were at the airport, and the woman sitting beside me was reading a book. Scott saw my eyes light up. He knows what a book nerd I am. He looked at me and said, "Don't even think about it." We laughed because I would have been perfectly fine engaging with this stranger about a book I hadn't even read, and he wanted me to focus on the conversation between us. I'm just one of those people who love people.

Nothing energizes me more than connecting with people. But as much as I love relationships, there's something else I love just about as much. You see, I also love a good to-do list. I'm the queen of writing it out just so I can go back to cross it off when it's done. Of course, there's nothing wrong with this! The problem comes when these two things merge—when I start putting my people on my to-do list.

A friend admitted once that she felt like she was simply an action step on my list. She had just moved to my town, and while I worked to introduce her to people I thought would make good friends, she was hurt because she felt like an item on my to-do list instead of a friend in a real relationship with me. I didn't realize I had done that. To me, I was helping her find connection. I wanted her to be happy and find friends who had kids the same age as hers. But she began feeling like just another task to mark off on my list.

Was that easy to hear? Not at all! But I'm glad she told me. Once I saw that tendency in my actions with her, I saw how easy it is for me to do this with everyone.

Hang out with kids. Check.

Text friend. Check.

Sit and watch a show with the kids or with Scott. Check.

Experience intimacy with my husband. Check.

If I'm not careful, my relationships can start to feel like things to check off my to-do list, things to *do* to keep connection alive. Keeping connection alive is good, but I have to be careful not to be motivated by the to-do list.

How do I do this?

I check my motivation. Am I reaching out because it's something on my to-do list? Or am I reaching out because I truly want to check on someone or see someone? Instead of rushing to the next item, now when I see someone, I make sure to give them my full attention. That's what it takes to build connection. No doing things just for the sake of doing them. No moving through the day doing stuff *for* people but forgetting to *be with* people.

This is a hard one for me. I usually can give all my attention to a friend over coffee, but by the end of the day, I struggle to give my full attention to Scott or the kids. I have to make an effort to put away my phone and focus on them fully.

I have to remind myself that efficiency isn't the goal. Efficiency doesn't build connection. Making sure that my girls don't experience FOMO or have arrived at all their activities doesn't build connection. Efficiency and productivity aren't the goals in my relationships; connection is.

> **E**fficiency and productivity aren't the goals in my relationships; connection is.

Have Fun

Think back to some of the best memories you've had with your family. They likely revolve around something fun, like a vacation, a holiday, or a family tradition. There's just something about fun that makes a moment stick.

My childhood was a lot of fun. We took yearly vacations to the beach. On the car rides there, my grandmother used to pack a brown paper bag with wrapped goodies, one to open for each hour of the drive. At home, I remember playing Nerf Ping-Pong on the dining room table when I was a teenager and spending evenings shooting hoops outside in the driveway. Fun was in our family DNA, especially when it came to traditions. My extended family would gather for holidays, and given that everyone loved sports, we always played a game. For Easter, it was always croquet. For Fourth of July, it was always Wiffle ball. For Thanksgiving, it was football. And that, my friends, is where the Washington Family Turkey Bowl was born.

When I was little, the Washington Family Turkey Bowl

consisted of two teams: me, my dad, and one of my cousins against my brother and the other cousin. We'd play for what felt like hours in the front yard of my grandmother's house. Over the years, this game has grown. Once grandkids entered the scene, the tradition took on a life of its own. Now a Thanksgiving Turkey Bowl Parade happens before the game. Keep in mind, this parade happens on my family property, where more people are in the parade than watching it. Makeshift floats are created, and Sinclair even rode her horse in the parade one year. There's a grand marshal, baton twirlers, and even a Turkey Bowl queen. (For the record, I've never been queen, and yes, it is a sore subject.) If you ask my kids what the most fun thing we do as a family is, they would probably say the Washington Family Turkey Bowl.

When it comes to family, fun matters. Fun has a way of quieting worry long enough to build connection. And I don't know about you, but as a parent, connection is definitely something I could use more of!

In 2022 we decided to deliberately build more fun into our family life. Our girls had never been to a concert, so we purchased tickets to see one of our favorite artists, Billie Eilish. We made a whole experience of it. We booked a hotel in Atlanta, ate at one of our favorite restaurants, and soaked up the fun and collective joy at the concert. Our fun year didn't end there. For spring break, we took the girls out west. We went to the Grand Canyon and then drove to Las Vegas to see Katy Perry perform. This trip will likely live on as one of our favorite experiences.

Of course, fun doesn't have to exist only in grand gestures or big trips. We try to do something fun in our house weekly. Often that includes doing something together like a hike or an activity. Sometimes we play tennis or pickleball. The point is to do something together, putting aside the everyday stresses and worries. Why? Because fun builds connection.

I know I've talked a lot about worrying about my kids, but I also worry about Scott. He's the most important person to me, so naturally I want to make sure he's okay too. I want to make sure we build connection over time and strengthen our relationship so that when the inevitable fractures happen and hurt is inflicted, connection isn't lost forever.

So just as we've been intentional about having fun with our kids, we have also made a point to have fun in our marriage. In some seasons, we've found it harder to do that than in others, but even when our kids were little, we made occasional date nights a priority. We would hire a babysitter and sneak away for dinner. Going out isn't cheap, but it's worth it. The investment in each other is crucial. I know that finding time in your schedule and money in the budget for a date isn't easy. Having fun together doesn't have to be expensive, though. It could be taking a walk after dinner or doing a hobby together. Maybe it's just working on a puzzle or watching a show. But fun usually does require a plan and some effort. It doesn't usually just happen.

Think about the last time you and your partner spent quality time together. How long ago was it? If it's been longer than a month, then put something on the calendar now. Paying attention to the frequency of your time together is a healthy practice.

Do you know why else we need fun? Fun is proven to lessen stress and to help us sleep better. It is also proven to strengthen relationships. Fun comes in all shapes and sizes. These are the years to build connection with our kids through fun. When you lie awake at night and worry if they're okay, think about the fun you have with them. Consider what you can do to have more fun. It doesn't have to be trips across the country. It can be game nights or family hikes. And these are the years to have fun with your partner. Spend time together, talk to each other, get to know who they are becoming. Do something that makes you laugh together. I've found that the more fun we have, the less worry keeps me up at night.

Practice Good Communication

Not only does having fun ease our worries and build connection, but communicating well does too. How do we know that our people are okay if we don't talk about it? A lot of communication is involved in building connection in this season of life. Of course, good communication doesn't necessarily equal number of words spoken. I'm not sure about your house, but our house has no shortage of words—everyone has something to say. So much so that sometimes I just drive alone in silence because my ears can't take another word!

All joking aside, talking to each other builds connection, and the more connected we feel, the less we worry. Giving your full attention when a family member is talking does a lot to strengthen the connection. When Scott talks about his day, his highs and lows, I want to pay attention. I try to be mindful of where he's at and what he's feeling. I've hurt his feelings at times by picking up my phone and texting someone while he's talking (hello, efficiency getting in the way again). Making eye contact and paying attention go a long way.

The same with my girls. I want to be mindful and aware of the world they live in. I want to ask questions and help them navigate their daily lives with wisdom. Some days I'm ready for bed by 9:00 p.m., exhausted from communicating. But I have to remind myself that it's part of building connection.

Some conversations aren't easy and are rather awkward. But caring enough about the connection to have the conversation is an investment in the relationship. It shows you care. It shows you love. We've had some hard and awkward conversations now that we are raising teenage girls. Avoiding them would have been easier. But having conversations—easy or hard ones—only strengthens the relationship. It reminds us that we are a team, that we are in this together.

One of the greatest phrases and tools I've learned in the last few years is in regard to communication. As much of a communicator as I am, I don't love hard conversations or confrontation. I'd rather run away. But Brené Brown said something about having difficult conversations that has changed my life. It has made me a better human, better mother, and better wife. She said, "I'm here to get it right, not be right."

When I enter a hard conversation, I remember that phrase. I say it over and over in my head. "I'm here to get it right, not be right." That helps me keep connection in mind. It helps me keep our future in mind. It helps me have perspective, empathy, compassion, and curiosity. Being right doesn't always build connection. But trying to get it right does.

Will my family be okay?

I hope so. I will keep showing up and trying to get it right. I will keep doing all I can to build a more secure connection.

When you worry about your family, I want you to answer these questions:

Am I staying engaged or trying to be efficient?
Am I paying attention or rushing through the relationship?
Am I making room for fun in my family?
Am I communicating in healthy, honest ways?

I think that's what it comes down to—building connection over time. Again, there are no guarantees in parenting or marriage; connection is built by being engaged and paying attention. It's built by showing up, having fun, and being intentional with people.

6
CHAPTER

what if . . . ?

Because our kids are currently at different schools that start at the same time, Scott and I divide and conquer. Somehow, I drew the short end of the stick and have to drive Rory to the farthest school every morning. Honestly, I'm not complaining, because I enjoy the extra minutes alone with her in the car. Quality time with each kid sometimes comes primarily in the form of drive time to and from activities. What I've learned in these years of parenting is that some of the best conversations happen while in motion.

As we drove to school one chilly November morning, Rory spoke up about something that I could tell had been on her mind just waiting to escape. We weren't two minutes into our drive when she said, "I felt fat yesterday." Given my history with body image issues, my insides tensed like I was about to jump off a cliff. My brain scrambled to find the right words to say. The good news? I've worked hard on keeping my outside calm even when my insides are scrambling. So I'm fairly certain Rory didn't see my internal panic.

She went on to say it was because there was a boy at school who weighed nearly twenty pounds less than her and all the other girls seemed tinier too. I knew how she felt. I remember a traumatic time in sixth grade when each kid had to step on a scale in the middle of PE class so the teacher could record our weight for the President's Physical Fitness Challenge. That day, I stepped on the scale in front of the other kids to see I weighed over a hundred pounds—116 to be exact. Funny how when something feels so traumatic, you can remember every detail of the moment. I remember what I was wearing. I remember who was there. I remember the number flashing on the scale. And I remember being so embarrassed thinking I had to be the largest kid in the class.

As she sat beside me in the car that day, I saw myself in Rory. I have been in her shoes, feeling those exact feelings. She's a year older than I was when it started for me. Since she'd just had a doctor's appointment, I knew her weight was just fine. But I also knew the angst she felt, the concern, the worry.

As we pulled up to school, I tried to encourage her. I told her what I wish I had understood during those years. Everyone's bodies are changing, growing, developing. It happens at a different time and pace for every person.

Later that morning I sat in my therapist's office. I'm seeing this therapist specifically to work through my issues and thoughts about my body. Though I've dealt with these issues for many years, I realized recently that I had never done real work to process that humiliating experience with the scale all those years ago. I just moved past it, never fully processing it, and eventually found myself wondering why I still struggled with similar thoughts and issues even in midlife. I mean, how many times have I uttered the exact phrase Rory did? *I feel fat.*

My therapist offered me some advice on what to say to her (and myself!) in those moments.

"Fat is not a feeling," she said gently.

I sat there like a deer in the headlights. All my life, I had thought fat was a feeling. Every other day, I felt fat. And if I felt it, it must be true. But it turns out she's right! Fat is in fact not a feeling. It's definitely never been on any feelings wheel I've ever seen.

She went on to talk about the importance of pointing that out to Rory too. She encouraged me to ask her to dig deeper, to ask herself what she may really be feeling when she feels fat. And to ask myself the same thing! We have to look underneath to see what we really feel so that we can deal with it adequately. We have to address the root issue if we ever want to be okay with ourselves.

What do I really feel when I say I feel fat? Embarrassment? Shame? Self-loathing?

As someone who struggles to feel her feelings, I have a hard time with this exercise. I tend to *think* my feelings rather than *feel* them. I can recognize that I might feel fear, but then I go into move-on mode. Once I've recognized it, I move on. This is where resources like therapy and books can be helpful. They help me pay attention to the feelings instead of just moving on.

I'm learning that I have to start with becoming emotionally literate, which often involves the reckoning I don't want to do. I want to skip that part. I want to believe that simply acknowledging the feeling is enough. But if I don't want it to resurface in the middle of my sleepless nights, I have to deal with it. I have to *feel* it.

Again, I asked myself that question: What do I really feel when I say I feel fat? The more I sat with it, the clearer the answer became.

What do I really feel when I say I feel fat?

Fear.

I'm afraid that I will be rejected. I'm afraid that no one will love me. I'm afraid that I won't be successful. I'm afraid that I won't belong. I'm afraid that if I lose control and gain weight, then all those nightmares will happen.

I am wrapped up in fear.

If we aren't aware, fear can hijack our well-being. Fear can take over the steering wheel and start driving the car. And before we know it, it leaves us consumed with anxiety in the middle of the night, wound up in a tight ball of fear.

In my deep dive into fear, I've discovered a question that we're really asking when we feel fear:

What if . . . ?

That question stems from the uncertainty we feel about life. Somewhere along the way, we came to believe that life was supposed to be certain, that there were clear answers to every problem. But we've lived long enough now to know that's not true. No matter how much we push for certainty, this world will never provide it. So we wonder, "What if . . . ?"

I don't know about you, but I'd love to turn off the chorus of what-ifs in my mind. I'd love to keep it from waking me up for another sleepless night. So what can we do to get there?

I've found that it starts by simply acknowledging the fear.

Become an investigator of your feelings. Dig underneath that initial question to find what is really going on inside you. It's practicing what my therapist advised: get at what you are really feeling underneath the question. When you're awake and wondering a what-if of your own, get curious. Ask yourself what you're really afraid of. Become an investigator of your feelings. Dig underneath that initial question to find what is really going on inside you.

What if I fail?

I'm afraid of looking like I'm not good enough, talented enough, or popular enough to be accepted.

What if my daughter isn't accepted?

I'm afraid of her feeling unwanted or unlovable.

What if they reject me?

I'm afraid of being judged.

Most recently, the question I've been digging into is a super practical and unique one that I didn't see coming.

What if Sinclair can't keep her horse at this barn?

Horses have been a part of our lives for many years now. Sinclair started riding around the age of eight, but her love for horses started as early as I can remember. Her whole life seemed to involve them. She always picked them as stuffed animals. Her sheets had horses all over them. The art on her walls featured horses. From as early as I can remember, she has named every horse we've ever seen (even the ones we simply drove past). And yes, she always remembered their names.

I never imagined owning horses. It seemed far-fetched.

But once we moved out of the suburban city life of the Atlanta area to the rural hills of Tennessee, owning horses became a reality. We bought two horses to live on our property. We had hoped they would be good for riding, specifically riding in shows, but we quickly realized that their days of showing were over. So while we intended to buy a horse for Sinclair to show, these horses proved to be more pet than prize pony.

The thing about riding is that it's not often a school sport. So Sinclair spends her time after school at a barn instead of on the school tennis courts. And given that she is now a full-fledged high schooler, riding horses is clearly not just a phase. (For the record, I never thought it would be.) If you have raised teenagers, specifically girls, then you might know the thoughts and fears that ran through our minds at the start of this season of life.

What if she falls into the wrong crowd?

What if she loses interest in school?

What if she gets into serious trouble?

With all the fears and what-ifs swirling in our minds, there was one big question we wanted to address: How can we occupy Sinclair's time, energy, and heart so that she doesn't get wrapped up in boys?

That's how Jax (short for Apple Jacks), horse number three, came into the picture.

We started shopping for a horse in the summer of 2022. Horse shopping at that time was a lot like the used car or housing market. Everything was selling fast and high. You could hardly send an interest email before the horse was already sold. After a failed attempt to even get on a waitlist for one particular horse, I knew I would have to act fast moving forward.

One day, the cutest Appaloosa horse popped up on my Facebook feed from the horse broker I was following. (That's a strange reality. I have a horse broker.) I reached out immediately, and by the next morning, Sinclair and I were driving four hours to try out this horse. She fell in love (because she's never met a horse she didn't love), and within hours, we had purchased Jax. Talk about stressful. I have a hard enough time pulling the trigger to buy a sweater from Target. A giant purchase like a horse almost did me in!

When we got Jax home, we quickly realized that his backstory was more complicated than we thought. He arrived with terrible sores in his mouth, which made it painful for him to be ridden with a bit. We then learned that he likely had been handled quite harshly in his life before us, so he was nervous and tense around others. Within the first month of owning him, we took him to a show. We were told he had experience in showing, but that first show was a surprise to us all. Jax refused every single jump, to the point he was disqualified from the show. That wasn't what we hoped for.

We realized then that Jax was greener than we had been led to believe. Showing him at Sinclair's level was off the table for a while. So Sinclair had to decide what she wanted. Did she want a more seasoned and trained horse that she could start showing immediately? Or did she want a horse she could train to become a show horse? Spend a year training Jax? Or sell him to get a more experienced horse? Ultimately, Sinclair chose to train him.

They spent months working on trust. She would ride him with loose reins so that she didn't pull on his bit. It was her way of telling him that she wouldn't be rough with him. She learned how to communicate with him and how to control her own anxiety so that it wouldn't raise the anxiety in him. She learned how to be patient with him because he needed a little extra time to get used to his surroundings. It wasn't long before we saw confidence build in Jax. He quickly became the barn favorite. He loosened up. He relaxed. He trusted Sinclair.

Another show opportunity came a few months after the first one. This time the results were very different. Sinclair showed Jax in two jumping classes, and he took home first place in both! Things were going great! All those pesky fears and what-ifs I was dealing with regarding Sinclair and Jax seemed to die down.

For a while.

Unexpectedly, we found ourselves at a crossroads with Sinclair's horse. Jax lived at the barn where Sinclair rode since we didn't have enough room on our land. The barn experienced some changes, and it looked like we might have to move Jax to another barn. This unknown future caused me so much anxiety. Changing barns meant more expenses, a longer drive from home, and disconnection from friends.

What if Sinclair can't keep her horse at this barn?

Every night for weeks, I thought about it. When I got curious about why I was afraid of moving barns, I realized it was about much more than Jax. I wasn't afraid of moving the horse; I was afraid of Sinclair losing her connection to him, her trainer, and her friends. Once I figured that out,

I was able to see the issue a little more clearly. Addressing the issue required being curious about what was causing the fear.

I intentionally gave you that seemingly "silly" what-if because I think many of you have similar concerns. But even if they seem silly, that doesn't mean they aren't valid. No matter how big or small your what-ifs seem, they're very real to you. This one certainly was to me!

What's tricky about managing our fears is that fear has to have a place in our lives. Fear is a necessary and valid emotion. If we never felt fear, then we might do some crazy, destructive, and unsafe things. Attempting to quiet our worries isn't about getting rid of our fear, it's about learning what to do with it.

I explained fear to my girls when they were younger by saying that fear is like an indicator light in the car. As we were driving to school one day, I pointed out the check engine light. I explained that the light comes on to indicate that something is potentially wrong with the car. Fear does the same for us! It gets our attention. It wants us to look around and make sure we are safe.

Sometimes we discover that our fears are unfounded—we are, in fact, safe. But other times we're not. And in those moments, when fear signals that we might be unsafe, we need to pay attention. Something may need to be addressed. So when you feel fear in any area of your life, pause and ask yourself a few questions.

Is what I'm afraid of true?
Does this need my attention?

Am I safe?

Is fear telling me something that can help me?

Let your answers determine what you do with your fear.

And remember this: Fear is an indicator, not a driver. It has a place in the car, but that place should not be in the driver's seat. We can't let it dictate, direct, or motivate our choices.

In 2016 Scott and I faced one of our biggest "face down in the dirt of the arena" moments. Do you know that reference? It pulls from a Theodore Roosevelt speech about daring greatly, facing critics, and rising up after falling. In the speech, he said that when you dare greatly, sometimes you will fall. Sometimes you will find yourself face down in the dirt. That's when you have to decide how to rise up. Face down in the dirt and unsure how to rise up—that's exactly where we were in that season.

I won't give the details of how we ended up face down in the arena because it isn't totally my story to tell. What I'll say in short is that we launched something and it failed. It didn't measure up to what we planned. And it left us face down in the arena of life, which isn't a fun place to be. The weeks after the failure were brutal.

Eventually, Scott came to me with a request: he wanted us to move. Rather than shut down his idea, I opened myself up to the conversation. That day, we talked honestly and compassionately about making a change for our family in this difficult season.

"I will consider moving if we're running toward something. But if we're running away, then I don't think it's the best idea," I finally told him.

I didn't want fear to be in the driver's seat. At the time, it felt like fear was screaming at us to run away. To hide. To get out of there. For us to move forward, whether we stayed put or moved away, we had to recognize the fears that were trying to drive us. We had to get them out of the driver's seat in order to make a wise decision.

In this world, we have a lot to be afraid of right now. So, yes, we need to pay attention to our fears. We need to get curious about them. But then we need to do a reality check.

For me, this starts with asking myself questions like these:

What situation is causing this fear?
What do I fear will happen?
What's the best that could happen?
What's the worst that could happen?
What would I tell a friend in the same scenario?

That last question is what always helps me most. Thinking about what I would say to a friend is the best reality check for me. In the face of their fears, I would offer compassion and kindness. But do I offer the same to myself? Not usually. Compassion is often hardest to give to ourselves. We think it's okay for someone else to receive compassion and empathy when they fail, but we find it terribly difficult to extend compassion to ourselves. Maybe that's shame whispering in our ears, yelling at us to do better, scolding us at each misstep. Shame always wants to make you feel like you are a bad human for what you did. Guilt says, "I did a bad thing." But shame says, "You are a bad thing." I would never look at a friend and express these words of shame. I would look at them with compassion and gentleness, knowing that a full story lay beneath the surface. Maybe it's time to start talking to ourselves the way we would talk to a friend.

Compassion is hard to give to ourselves, but it's needed when we're wrestling with a what-if.

Finally, we have to address our fears so they don't destroy our connections to the people who comfort, help, and strengthen us. Fear has a way of eroding those connections, of telling us to keep our vulnerability to ourselves. But because vulnerability is essential to connection, we have to be brave enough to open ourselves up.

What if they don't like me?

What if they reject me?

What if they think I'm weird?

Questions like that threaten our connections. They tempt us to avoid opening up to others. But remember, sharing yourself with another, facing fear, and feeling vulnerable all require a level of trust. That's an essential piece of connection. No, I'm not asking you to share all of yourself with everyone you encounter. Rather, I'm asking you to consider opening up to someone you trust. Remember, building trust is like building muscle. You have to flex it over and over. Acknowledging our fear and choosing to trust anyway is where connection starts.

After we purchased Jax, the broker reached out to ask permission to connect me with the family that lived next door to where Jax previously lived. Their daughter had grown quite attached to him in the time he was there. She was slightly younger than Sinclair, so the two of them became friends, bonding over their connection to this horse. Sinclair would often send her pictures and videos of Jax just to keep the two in touch. Fast-forward a few months, and they asked to come watch Sinclair show Jax. And by "come watch," I mean they drove four hours to see them compete.

As I stood with the mother at this show, she opened up about their experience with Jax. The girl's grandparents lived next door to the farm where Jax lived. They moved into the house because the grandfather was dying. This girl met Jax the week her grandfather died. The mother told me how Jax became a source of light, love, and peace for her daughter. She went on to tell me how Jax and his previous owner never connected. He would run from the owner when she would try to catch him out in the pasture. Somehow Jax connected with this little girl in a different way. In fact, Jax wouldn't let anyone pet him except this girl. Talk about trust!

As she told me this story, we were standing beside Jax while Sinclair sat on him waiting for her next class in the show. The mother was stroking Jax's face as tears welled up in her eyes.

"I can tell that he is so happy with Sinclair," she finally said. "He would never let me pet him before. He was nervous and distrusting, yet here he is letting me pet him."

Horses are incredible creatures. Their ability to feel is beyond my understanding. I'm blown away at how Jax knew this woman's daughter needed him. I'm blown away at how my daughter built trust with him over time. And I'm blown away at how those connections changed the way Jax trusted others.

Yes, fear can threaten our ability to trust. But when we address the cause of our fears, trust can be rebuilt. Connection can be made. Peace can be found.

So instead of allowing fear to erode connection, move toward connection and relationship. When you feel afraid, reach out to a trusted friend and let them know how you feel.

What I'm asking you to do isn't easy. I know because I'm doing the same thing. When the what-if questions overwhelm me, I do the work. I dig beneath the question and ask myself what I'm really feeling. I get curious about what I'm really afraid of. I recognize that fear and then I fact-check it. Opening up about my fear (especially to a therapist) has been hard but helpful. It's certainly better than letting the fear consume me, especially in the middle of the night when I'd rather be sleeping. And I most certainly don't like watching my daughter fear the same things I do. The more we do the work for ourselves, the more we can help our children learn how to do the work too.

do i matter?

I recently read a novel about being able to time travel back to a certain point in time—a time you would like to revisit and redo. Honestly, who hasn't wished for an opportunity like that a time or two?

In this season of life, I often find myself thinking about some of the significant choices I've made along the way. They run on replay in my mind around 3:00 a.m. Most often, they center on choices I've made in my career.

At night, my mind takes me all the way back to being a young college graduate just beginning my career. At that age, I didn't know what I wanted to do, but I took a job and that was a start. I took my love for baseball and combined it with my love for people and ended up as a marketing assistant for the Chattanooga Lookouts, a minor league baseball team for the Cincinnati Reds.

My days were spent organizing the gift shop and managing the mascot. I got to help coordinate community events and go to work at the ballpark every day. It's easy to romanticize parts of the past, so I'm sure when I look back on this job in the middle of the night, I'm doing a little bit of that. But in my haste to get somewhere fast—to get somewhere more noticeable, more meaningful—I quit after only a year.

That's the moment I would revisit. That's the moment I would go back and change.

Yes, I quit because I didn't enjoy what I was doing. I felt like my full potential wasn't being tapped into. But you know what? It was a start. Instead of realizing that, I had the idea that I was going to conquer the world right away. I had to do something big and significant even though I was just starting out. So instead of giving myself time to grow and develop, I quit.

I changed course. I went from working in baseball to working in the nonprofit world. Why? Because I was chasing passion. I was chasing purpose. In the late 1990s and early 2000s, there was a lot of talk about finding your passion and purpose. I listened to countless sermons and read books on what to do with your life. They all told me the same thing: you should feel a sense of purpose from your career.

If I could go back to that twentysomething girl deciding to leave her first job to chase some elusive sense of purpose, I would tell her that work is work. There are seasons when it's okay not to be super passionate about your work. It doesn't always need to feel like your purpose in life. Sometimes you work a job because you need to work. Knowing that would have helped to take the pressure off myself.

I'm fully aware that going back to change that one decision would alter every aspect of my life. Taking the path I did led me to being a writer and a podcaster. It led me to my husband, my kids. Obviously, I want all those things. What I want isn't to change where I ended up. What I want to change is my pursuit of purpose.

Purpose is on the long list of things I question and worry

about in the middle of the night. At this point in life, many of us have spent years, decades even, working in a certain direction. Maybe you've spent all that time working in a specific industry or for a certain company. It's easy to wake up one day in midlife and wonder if this is what you dreamed of all those years ago when you were bright-eyed and bushy-tailed. Is this really what life is supposed to be about?

For some, this is where the midlife crisis begins. I once heard someone describe this season of adulthood as the midlife malaise. When they said it, I had to look it up. *Malaise* means a general feeling of discomfort or an uneasiness whose exact cause is difficult to identify. It's a recurring sense of discontent. Yeah, that sounds about right. That sounds like right where I am. The existential question Scott and I constantly toss around in this season is this: "How can I be more content?" We have everything we need, but we still feel a sense of discontent.

Now what?

What does this all mean?

Does any of it matter?

Where do I go from here?

Am I successful?

I think we feel this sense of discontent with our work for several reasons. Can we just pause for a second and evaluate together? Maybe . . .

You haven't reached "success," at least in the way you define it.

You've stopped producing results.

You're bored with your daily rhythm.

You've been doing this for a long time.

You thought you signed up for something else.

You quit work to stay home, but that doesn't feel like your purpose.

You're no longer accomplishing anything.

If any of these statements describe your situation, I know how you feel. Life has a way of not turning out like we expected or hoped. It has a way of making us wonder if we've ever pursued the right direction for ourselves. For me, all those feelings and questions and statements boiled down to one question that rolls around in my head at night:

Do I matter?

I wrestled with this question earlier in life too. Almost the entirety of my twenties could be defined by my drive. I combined my drive with my belief that the world was my oyster. The result? I felt like I could do anything. I could go anywhere.

And for a while I did.

I achieved a lot in my twenties. I moved across the country to work for a megachurch that was known all across the world. I began a career in speaking and had many opportunities to travel and speak. I signed a book deal when I was only twenty-five years old. Anything seemed possible.

So imagine my surprise when I approached thirty and things weren't moving quite so fast. I lost my job and had my first child around the same time. Seemingly overnight, the world wasn't my oyster anymore. I no longer felt driven. I just felt lost. Without work—without success—did I have a purpose? Did I matter anymore?

Truth be told, I felt that way for a long time after thirty. Much of my time was spent wondering if I had peaked. Maybe I had accomplished everything I was going to accomplish in life. Of course I now know that's not true. But back then, I wasn't so sure. I struggled with apathy, discontent, and depression. I was left wondering if I still had a purpose to pursue.

Let me pose to you an interesting "would you rather" question that Rory recently asked me:

Would you rather make less money but be happy in your work or make more money but be unhappy in your work?

Pretty insightful question for a twelve-year-old, huh? I told her that my answer depends. For starters, truly considering that question is a privilege; not all of us get to choose a job with such freedom. Still, I told her that if I needed the money, it didn't matter how miserable the job was. We have bills to pay, and work is what pays them. No matter how you would answer that question, I think it cuts to the heart of what we feel in midlife when it comes to work—we feel torn between working with purpose and working from need.

Many of us wake up twenty years into a career only to realize we're burned out, weary from the work. Many of us have realized that our job won't give us what we wanted from the start. We chose our work because we were passionate about it. Maybe we even felt like it was our purpose. But now what?

I often wonder if our questions of passion and purpose

are distinctly American. If I had grown up in a different culture, would I be so obsessed with finding and living out my purpose? Purpose sells books, and it sells books because it's a tension we feel in this culture. We see someone who is filled with purpose, and we praise them. I once had someone compliment me, saying, "Even the way you walk is purposeful." Hilarious, right? In that moment, I actually didn't know where I was walking, but I walked as if I did. They didn't know that, of course. They just saw the appearance of purpose. And boy, in this country at least, we like to throw confetti for people who seem to have their purpose all figured out.

Can I propose a new question for us to consider: When did purpose become the goal?

I sat with a therapist one hot summer day and listed off all that had occurred in my life in the last two years alone. It was like a fire hydrant was opened and I couldn't be stopped. I went on and on about all I had done—everything from writing a book to moving states and everything in between. She said I was driven. That was interesting because, at the time, I didn't think of myself as driven. Sure, maybe I was driven in my twenties, but now? Now I felt lazy. I had written a book, launched a book, and moved our family. Yet somehow I felt lazy.

Her words made me realize that somewhere along the way, purpose began to feel like pressure.

Pressure to perform.

Pressure to produce.

Pressure to pursue purpose.

At this point in life, pressure seems to have a way of

making us want to quit. I recently read an Instagram post from a friend who is a floral artist. She's had great success in her industry, so her words surprised me a little.

"I no longer love flowers like I used to."

She went on to say that she wonders if she's in a midlife crisis herself. The thing she has loved—the thing that has given her both success and a great sense of purpose over the years—is the thing she's ready to give up. Maybe you can relate. I know I can! I think many of us have been striving toward a specific purpose for so long that we're stunned when we realize we're tired. We've been working toward that goal—that purpose—for decades. Now all we can think about is why it matters anymore.

Did I choose the wrong path? The wrong purpose?

Should I quit? Can I quit?

Do I matter anymore—especially if I quit?

Friend, you are not alone. It's normal to wonder if what you do matters. To wonder if you've pursued the right purpose for your life. To be weary and ready to quit. So what can we do when we feel that way?

Redefine Purpose

To begin, I think we have to redefine what purpose is. I grew up in a time when it was preached that your purpose is tied to your work in a significant way. I didn't realize the pressure it put on me as I entered the workforce. Purpose carried so much weight. If I didn't have that, I didn't have anything.

I once heard Elizabeth Gilbert talk about purpose and passion on a podcast.[8] I've listened to that episode several times just to keep it in mind. She talked about how she used to be such a preacher about passion and purpose until one day someone poked a hole in her thinking. She met a woman who said she tried to do everything that Elizabeth and others had suggested to find her purpose. But she had never uncovered a clear sense of purpose for herself. She felt so defeated. And every time someone like Elizabeth would preach about purpose and passion, she'd feel even worse. With that one conversation, Elizabeth began rethinking her beliefs about purpose and passion.

She followed with a story about walking down the street one day to come upon a man on a ladder working on a storefront. The ladder appeared to be a little wobbly, so Elizabeth was nervous the man might fall. Without his knowledge, she simply stood under the ladder and held it still until he began to come down. Before he even saw her, she walked away. What she did in that moment mattered.

It felt like purpose.

That story has stuck with me. Maybe purpose doesn't have to be saving the world. Maybe it could be as simple as saving a man from falling off a ladder. Purpose comes down to a desire to matter. The good news is, we were made to matter. We want to believe we are here on earth for a reason, and I think we are. But maybe that reason is something small. Maybe it's simple. Maybe it's ordinary.

So think about what you do that matters. It doesn't have to be big. It could be as simple as being the one who wakes up first and starts the coffee. You may scoff at that suggestion, but trust me, there is purpose to be found there. What if you found purpose and pleasure in that simple task? How would it change your outlook for the day? How would it change the way you viewed the people in your house planning to drink that coffee? How would it change your sense of accomplishment in your days?

When we see purpose as simply doing something that matters, it takes the pressure off. Because doing something that matters can exist outside of what you do for work. You may not feel like your job is purposeful at all. I think it's rare for someone to find work that gives them a deep, lasting sense of purpose. Most of the time, work is just work, but that doesn't mean you don't matter. Maybe you could find a sense of purpose beyond the actual work tasks. Maybe you matter because you improve the day of those you work with through simple acts of kindness.

I also suggest finding something that matters to you outside of work. It could be anything from the environment to family to friends to animals to art. Rory recently taught me how to turn plastic bags into sleeping mats for the homeless. Cutting up plastic bags, creating "yarn," and then weaving the pieces together matters.

When we see purpose as simply doing something that matters, it takes the pressure off.

If you feel like you're unsure of your purpose, look around to see ways you are already being useful or ways that you could be useful. You can find and make meaning in many ways, some of them very ordinary. Different seasons come with different opportunities. We need to find ways to pull our focus outward, not inward. Women, especially mothers, are already doing a million things that feel outward. We are quick to ignore ourselves. I'm not talking about doing more of that. I'm talking about doing something you find meaningful.

Let me give you an example of being useful.

I got a scholarship to play tennis in college. I don't tell many people that, mostly because I haven't played in over twenty years, which means I'm a little rusty, to say the least. When I graduated college, I graduated from tennis too. I hung up my racket and never went back, but watching Rory play this past year made my heart long to play again.

When you were really good at something in the past, trying it again is scary because you probably won't be as good as you were. And people may expect more of you and then judge you when you don't live up to that expectation. Nonetheless, I agreed to start playing tennis with my friend Hannah. And you know what? It was fun. Sure, I'm not as good as I was. I missed some shots, and my forehand needs a lot of work, but it was still fun.

At the same time, Sinclair started dating a boy on the high school tennis team, so we started spending afternoons at the tennis courts when he had a match. Their coach heard I played tennis, and the other day he sat down by me and said, "How's your tennis game?"

Me: Um, I haven't played in over twenty years, but doing pretty good given that.

Coach: Would you be able to come play a match

against our number one girl? She doesn't have
much competition on our team.

Me: [wide-eyed blinks]

I wanted to say yes because that sounded fun. I'd been
so excited to start playing again. But I was scared to death.
Scared to look silly, like a fool. Scared this girl and coach
would wonder why they ever thought to ask me. But then
I remembered that this could be an opportunity to matter—to be useful.

Me: Yes, I'd love to play her. I'll either give her
some competition or make her feel good about
herself. Either way is a win for her.

Monday rolled around, and as the clock inched toward
four, I found myself wanting to bail, to find an excuse not to
show up. I felt tired (which is often the norm for this stage
of life). So I poured a cup of coffee, put on some music to get
me going, and then walked out the door. Showing up is the
hardest part. I never felt more my age than I did walking up
to those courts full of teenagers.

I wish I could tell you that I played the most amazing
game of tennis that day. I wish I could tell you that she
was blown away by my ability. But I can't. She wiped the
floor with me. There were many times that I just stood
flat-footed and watched as the ball whizzed by me. I felt
defeated afterward, but not because I lost. I wrestled with
my shame, which told me that I shouldn't have tried. But
after processing those emotions, I landed in a better place.

I was useful that day. I gave her someone new to play. I gave her some competition, and I also boosted her confidence. I was useful. I mattered. Pay attention to what makes you feel like you matter. Find meaning and purpose in that.

Take the Pressure Off

In many ways, we've treated finding our purpose like finding our soulmate. I remember feeling pressure to find "the one." I grew up thinking there was one person made just for me who, when I found them, would complete me. (Insert in your mind the image of Jerry Maguire here.) That would be the person I was destined to marry. As I grew up, I came to realize that wasn't the case. And when I took the pressure off finding "the one," I relaxed and enjoyed myself instead of worrying about dating to find "the one." I think the same is true with finding purpose. You weren't born with one purpose that you have to find at all costs. You won't miss it if you don't follow some perfect formula. Take the pressure off.

If you don't remember anything else you read today, remember this: you matter. Your existence alone gives you purpose, and that truth can take the pressure off. Look around and see where you are needed. Maybe it's as simple as holding a ladder. Maybe it's picking up your kids—and sometimes even your neighbor's kids—during carpool in the afternoon. Maybe it's making sure to say hi to people when you are in the office. Maybe it's finding a way to do something kind for your partner. Boil it down to something simple. Focus on those simple acts of purpose—those simple acts of mattering. When we do that, the pressure comes off. We redefine purpose as simply finding ways to matter. Then we can navigate what we do in life or work from a more relaxed state. Because purpose is no longer a one-time thing to find—it's something to discover on an ongoing basis.

Find Gratification

Finding happiness in what we do for work is different from finding purpose there. For instance, I have a job as an editor. It's a skill I've developed over the last nearly twenty years. It's a job that pays the bills. I'm not passionate about it. It doesn't get me up in the morning. At times, I've wanted to quit. But I've realized I have a lot of moments of satisfaction in that job. For one, it affords me the opportunity to connect with others. I get to help other people develop their writing projects. But it also gives me the opportunity to do something I'm good at, and I find satisfaction in that. Sometimes we just need to do something we are good at. In some seasons, purpose can be that simple.

And if purpose can be that simple, maybe contentment is closer than we think in many areas of our lives—work included! Research shows that if you engage with your strengths, you'll find more gratification in work. Somewhere—whether in your personal life or work life—do something you are good at. The more you utilize your strengths, the more gratification you will find. And if you find gratification, you'll shift into a more positive mindset.

I thought a lot about gratification when we moved to

Tennessee and decided to get horses. When we said yes to acquiring two horses, our property wasn't ready for them. We worked on the weekends to build a beautiful wooden fence. Trust me when I say it was definitely work.

Then the horses arrived.

Confession: I didn't know the horses would poop as much as they did. When I drove past horse pastures, I never noticed piles of poop. But our pasture quickly became just that: piles and piles of poop. Turns out, you have to walk around the pasture and either shovel up the poop or spread it out. So, every day, I took my pitchfork and walked the pasture kicking poop.

Did I enjoy this? No.

Did I want to quit my editing job to work on a farm? No.

But was it gratifying? Yes.

Kicking poop was a little bit like Elizabeth Gilbert holding that ladder. It was a simple task, but I was qualified to do it. It was work that reminded me that I'm needed here. I matter here. In moments when my paying job doesn't feel that way, it's nice to find other tasks that provide that sense of gratification.

Pause, Pivot, or Quit

Of course, we can't talk about feeling purposeless at work without being real about the fact that sometimes there's a reason. Maybe you feel discontent with your job. Maybe you wonder if this is all you'll ever do in life and every day is a struggle just to show up and find anything satisfying.

What then?

This is when you should get curious. (If you haven't noticed, the last few years of my life have been marked by two big things: curiosity and horses.) Our family had a banner custom-made for us with the phrase "Be Curious." Maybe it's time for you to get curious and ask why you feel this way about your work.

Why do you feel discontent in what you do?

Why do you feel a lack of purpose in what you do?

Why do you feel like you have peaked?

The answers to those questions will help you decide what comes next. In my mind, there are three possible next steps: pause, pivot, or quit. After wrestling with those questions, maybe the best thing for you to do is simply pause. That means not making any moves. Maybe simply pausing and being aware of your feelings is the best place to be. Being aware is being open to other ideas and opportunities. It's being honest about where you are and how you feel. Sometimes that's enough.

Or maybe the best thing for you to do is pivot. (I can't write that word without envisioning Ross from *Friends* yelling, "Pivot!" as they carry a sofa up the stairs.) Simply redirect. Imagine you're using the Waze app and you've found a different route to take. So you pivot. You change course. You take a new path because now that's the best path for you. Purpose works in a similar way. It's not about the destination or the outcome; it's about having a target, a plan, a reason why. It doesn't have to be written in permanent marker. It can be subject to change as seasons and circumstances change. A pivot will look different for everyone. Scott pivoted from working for himself for most of his career to working for a publicly traded company. He still worked in the video-creation field, but pivoting to working for a company alleviated some of the stress that working alone brought. Years ago, I pivoted from simply writing curriculum to managing the process of curriculum creation. It was still in a field I knew, but the pivot allowed me to expand and tap into other skills. So if you find yourself in a position to pivot, maybe it's time to make the move.

Finally, maybe the best thing to do is quit. Maybe what you do is creating too much discontent, apathy, or depression in your life and the best thing to do is leave. Let me be the loudest voice in the room to shout: it's okay to quit something!

In the last few years, I've been faced with multiple opportunities to quit. I've bumped up against the reality that something isn't working or that I've outgrown something. This includes everything from work to faith to relationships. I mean, can we all collectively agree that the past few years have been a lot? I know many people who have turned their lives upside down since 2020, and I mean turned them upside down on purpose.

For us, that change came when we decided to leave our Mayberry of a town outside of Atlanta to move back to my hometown in Tennessee. I had never planned on moving back. I have always been one to fly the coop. I moved to California when I was twenty-one and moved to Georgia to live on my own at twenty-four. I never imagined going back.

But after the shutdown of 2020, we recalibrated our values. We looked toward the next phase of parenting and life to see what we would need. With those things in sight, we moved to Tennessee to be near my parents' farm. We nestled onto about three acres of land (which, after living in the city, felt like eighty acres!). We felt like we lived in wide-open spaces (cue the Dixie Chicks). With that, I think our eyes were bigger than our stomachs. Because shortly after we moved, we were offered those two horses I told you about.

We didn't know what we were getting into with horses. Things were fine for a while, but the horses quickly burned through our land. Like, literally. They ate every inch of grass in the pasture. Did you know that cows simply graze on grass, but horses pull the grass up by the root? Neither did I! By winter, some six months later, the pasture was all dirt. Every time it rained, our land was a mud pit.

All of life since moving has been a lot. We've had to juggle the move, different schools, and new work, just to name a few of the stress points. So in the middle of it all, I asked my husband what I could do to help alleviate some stress.

"Get rid of the horses."

Imagine my face.

Blank stare. A few dramatic blinks.

"Okay . . ."

I just sort of set that aside. I took that comment under review and decided to wait and see if he still felt that way six months later.

Time marched on until about six months later, in another moment of trying to help my husband manage stress, I asked again, "What can I do to help?"

"Get rid of the horses," came his reply.

I knew that's what I needed to do. I reached out and tried to find someone to take on two retired horses. The problem is that retired horses are like deadweight. They are expensive yard decorations, and most people don't want the added stress and expense. To me, giving them away felt like quitting. I felt shame about it. I felt like people would see that we couldn't really manage horses, and I didn't like that feeling.

I didn't want to be a quitter.

Not only did I feel like a quitter for wanting to get rid of our horses, but I felt like a quitter because I stopped my podcast. I knew I needed a break and that the break could turn into something permanent. But how was I supposed to quit something that informed so much of my worth?

And on top of that? I realized it was time to quit some relationships. I loved these people, but I realized the relationships had served their purpose and it was time to move forward. It might not have been a dramatic ending, but nonetheless, it felt like quitting.

That season taught me that it's okay to quit. Quitting something isn't the same as being a quitter. Quitting is an action; quitter is an identity. Just because I decide it's time to quit something doesn't mean I am now classified as a quitter. Rather, I am classified as someone who is finally confident enough to make a hard choice. Someone who isn't afraid to live with the fallout.

I want the same to be true for you! If your best next step is to quit, then take that step. This is where wrestling with your

Just because I decide it's time to quit something doesn't mean I am now classified as a quitter. Rather, I am classified as someone who is finally confident enough to make a hard choice. belief about purpose is so important. If you believe your purpose is tied solely to your work, then quitting might be really hard. But if you have shifted your understanding of purpose to be about more than just your work, you'll realize there are a million other ways to matter in this world and maybe you need to quit in order to find them. Just a note on quitting work: Sometimes we can't quit our job because we have bills to pay. So maybe the first step in quitting is simply starting to look for something else. And as you investigate the options, find ways to matter outside of work.

Let's come back to this idea that purpose can be found in many small ways. If we can embrace that truth, maybe we'll find ourselves sleeping more peacefully instead of chasing the peak we'll never reach. Jonathan Haidt is a social psychologist and one of my favorite authors. In his book *The Happiness Hypothesis*, he says, "Love and work are crucial for human happiness because, when done well, they draw us out of ourselves and into connection with people and projects beyond ourselves."[9] Find something that draws you out of yourself and into connection with others, even if that isn't your work. Find something, anything. Big or small. Ordinary even. Do it to remind yourself that you matter.

Do I matter?

If I widen the lens and see this concept from a new perspective, then yes, I do matter. I do have purpose. I've just redefined my view of purpose. I've taken the pressure off. And I've started to find fulfillment, contentment, and gratification in small actions that matter.

do i still believe in this?

Growing up in a small town in southeastern Tennessee, I was no different from most of the people around me. Most families spent a lot of their lives at church. If the doors were open, we were there. That is just what we did. My adolescent years were spent in Sunday school, youth group, youth choir, mission trips, and church camps. I could likely write an ode to 1990s youth group.

And I loved every minute.

Then a funny thing happened in my early twenties. Some of the faith traditions I'd grown up with didn't quite fit in the same way. I started to see things differently. Not drastically different, but different all the same. This on its own isn't shocking. Most people who grow up in Christian culture hit a point of doubt and uncertainty at some point in their faith journey.

The problem for me? I didn't know this was a normal part of growing up.

As it turns out, around the time they head to college, most people seem to challenge what they grew up believing. I didn't get that memo. So upon graduating high school, I stepped right into attending a Christian college. I chose a place that affirmed everything I believed up to that point. I chose a place where I thought my beliefs would be safe and secure, a place I thought would keep my Christianity (or at least the version of it I knew at the time) fully intact.

I wasn't looking to grow in my faith. I welcomed the safe bubble—a place where my faith was reinforced instead of challenged.

My parents became followers of Jesus when they were adults. Though they grew up in church, their relationship with Jesus started in their twenties—as adults. This isn't surprising given the time period in which they were living. Their coming-of-age years were in the mid- to late 1970s when the Jesus movement was in full swing and evangelicalism was starting to boom. To my parents' credit, they challenged their beliefs and made their own decisions about faith. They were able to push against, ask questions about, and challenge some of how they were raised. As a result, they went from cultural Christians to evangelical Christians.

In other words, they started following Jesus in a real way.

The irony is that those of us raised by parents who chose evangelicalism in their young adult lives didn't really get the same choice to figure it out for ourselves. We were raised in our parents' way of thinking and beliefs from the moment we were born.

We grew up going to church every Sunday morning.

We lived for vacation Bible school every summer.

We went to Wednesday night youth group without fail.

We traded our summer days for summer church camps.

And it didn't end there.

Many of us, like me, went to Christian universities, or got involved in parachurch organizations (which were on the rise by the time we entered college), or started serving in the church right after graduation. We were encouraged to go deeper in our faith commitments in every part of our lives. For us, church wasn't supposed to be just a part of life; it was supposed to be all of life.

Of course, as we grew up, our brains developed and we could think for ourselves. That's where things got sticky because we'd grown up hearing that asking questions or doubting or changing our minds on something was a sign of a lack of faith. Our faith was supposed to be solid, certain, secure, unwavering. Those of us midlifers who grew up in a faith tradition like this didn't feel we had permission to change our minds, ask questions, or express doubt over anything we believed.

And then came deconstruction.

Honestly, I don't like that word. Maybe it came about in a genuine conversation about navigating changes in beliefs, but now it just feels like something that someone wants to capitalize on or argue about. In faith circles like the one I grew up in, deconstruction is looked upon negatively. But while I may not love the word itself, for me, the process of deconstruction has been positive.

My favorite thing to order at Chipotle (where I am a regular customer) is a burrito bowl. Rice, beans, chicken, veggies, cheese, guacamole (yes, I'm willing to pay extra for the guac)—it's everything I love about a burrito but packaged in a different way. If someone hadn't thought to deconstruct that burrito—if they hadn't broken it down and put it back together in a new way—we would never have experienced the beauty that is the burrito bowl.

While I know the stakes are higher with our faith, I do

think the same principle is true. Deconstruction is simply taking the pieces apart and assembling them in another way, seeing if there are other ways of understanding our faith. It's reconfiguring a puzzle while still taking that puzzle seriously. The Bible—which our Christian faith is based on—requires a lot of interpretation. What does its teaching mean for today? What did it mean then? How should I read it? That's why we have so many denominations, so many different faith traditions. And each faith tradition has interpreted (assembled) the "ingredients" from the Bible in a slightly different way.

But since some see deconstructing faith as a bad thing, let's think of our faith journey as evolving. To me, deconstructing feels like taking something apart, while evolving feels like growing upon. That more accurately describes what's happened with my faith.

As I mentioned, I chose a Christian college, and then I chose church ministry as a profession when I was a mere twenty-two years old. I started my career at a globally known megachurch that was described as "seeker sensitive." Back then this was a new concept, especially for someone who grew up in small-town Tennessee—the belt buckle of the Bible Belt. I devoted my time to writing devotionals, leading small groups of teenage girls, and traveling the world to speak at Christian events. I went to seminary and earned a master of arts in biblical studies, and I eventually went on to work for a company that writes curriculum for churches. Everything I did for work or fun was connected to my Christian faith. I ate, drank, and slept faith. I was deeply involved in all things Christian.

While I was living, working, and showing up in those faith spaces, my actual faith was evolving. Sometimes when we hear that someone's faith has evolved or been deconstructed, we imagine a dramatic 180-degree change. But most often it's just a gradual shift in thinking. For example, until I went to college, I had only ever really attended my home church, and I just assumed most churches believed the same things I believed. Maybe I was naive, but I assumed everyone interpreted the Bible the same way. So even though I attended a Christian college, the college was of a different denomination than my home church. Seeing the faith of others—similar yet different—allowed me the opportunity to look at what I thought was true and ask some questions.

The evolving of my faith didn't end there. I spent two summers working for a Christian camp in Panama City Beach, Florida, while I was in college. Here again, I was presented with people from various denominations and diverse viewpoints on aspects of faith. It was the first time I ever considered what someone who isn't a follower of Jesus might feel during a church service. This again gave me the opportunity to look at what I thought church was about and to ask questions about what I believed. These weren't monumental events that challenged my faith. They were just opportunities to see through different lenses. They were small moments of change. Small moments of evolution.

Widening my world widened my faith. It's easy to think the world is small when you never leave your surroundings. Leaving home afforded me the opportunity to meet other people, to experience other churches, and to see the way people outside my home church saw and lived their faith.

Having kids was a big catalyst in the evolution of my faith. I wanted to own what I believed if I was going to share it with my children. 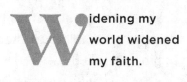 **Widening my world widened my faith.** I looked at stories in the Bible through the lens of how my kids would understand them. I looked at my own experiences to see how they lined up with some of the theology I had believed all my life. And slowly my faith evolved. Even the way I read the Bible slowly changed. I started to think that maybe there wasn't just one way to read the Scriptures. Maybe my denomination hadn't cornered the market in interpretation. That may not blow your mind, but it blew mine.

Let me give you an example.

I've always loved a great story. Who doesn't, really? The outline of a great story always involves a protagonist and a foe—a bully or an enemy, someone who is out to destroy the protagonist. In other words, all great stories have both a hero and a villain.

I am the protagonist of my life. It's my story that I'm writing. And often when I face adversity or someone who hurts my happiness or peace or success, I look around for the villain—someone who is out to destroy me, to get in my way, or to ruin my happiness, peace, or success.

In other words, I look for someone to blame.

Someone to blame for my unhappiness.

Someone to blame for the current state of my career.

Someone to blame for my lack of motivation.

Someone to blame for my evolving faith.

In Christian circles, it's easy to pin everything on the devil. That's our ultimate villain, right? When struggle happens, whether in circumstances or in our hearts, we want to pin it on that devil.

The devil made me do it.

I've given the devil a seat at the table.

The devil is coming for me hard this week.

If I'm honest, I have said those things in the past. And if I'm especially honest, I usually said them as a way to put blame somewhere other than on me, or to try to make sense out of something that wasn't working out, or to explain why I continued to struggle in some way.

However, as my faith has evolved, I've learned to see the source of my unhappiness in a new way. I realized it wasn't the devil destroying my life. It wasn't the devil creeping into my relationship and causing unrest. It wasn't the devil making the bad decision that led to a lot of heartache. It wasn't the devil making me impatient with my kids.

I'd ask you to consider the same question: When it comes to your happiness, who do you think is the real villain?

When you feel anger toward your partner or child . . .

When you open up Instagram and immediately resent what you see . . .

When you feel unworthy of love because of something you've done in the past . . .

When you feel afraid to be the real you in front of friends . . .

When you feel like you're not enough . . .

When you feel like you aren't capable of chasing that dream . . .

When you wish you could turn back time and make a different choice . . .

Think about it. Who is making those choices, or grappling with those feelings, or struggling through those circumstances? The person who ends up stealing much of my well-being is me. It's the girl staring back in the mirror. And I think the same could be true for you.

The devil doesn't have a pitchfork and wear a red suit. The devil likely wears something from Target that she bought while sipping a cappuccino aimlessly walking around the store accumulating items in her cart that she never knew she needed. That's me. I'm raising my hand. Guilty as charged.

I'm not saying that I am evil or that you are evil. And this isn't a debate about whether a devil is out there serving as an enemy. I'm saying that when we want to point a finger of blame, the finger often needs to point toward ourselves. Sometimes the devil wears Target.

Our faith needs room to breathe, move, and evolve.

Twenty years ago, this thought would've seemed crazy to me. But today, as my faith has evolved, I've come to see it in a new way.

Our faith needs room to breathe, move, and evolve. Our faith needs to be pushed and pulled. Growth happens in that place of tension.

The longer I walked in my faith, the more questions

seemed to come up. Sometimes I faced those questions with a welcoming smile, and other times those questions caused anger. At the time, I didn't want my faith to evolve. I didn't want it to be challenged. Why? Because I had received the message that changing your mind wasn't good. That thinking critically about what you believed was bad. That simply asking a question was sinful.

That's how I found myself awake at night, worried over the question:

Do I still believe in this?

And this question quickly followed: What will happen if I change what I believe?

Let me tell you the most important thing I've learned as my faith has evolved: it is normal to change the way you think. It's a good and healthy practice for all of us. I believe this even more since becoming a mother and raising my girls. I really hope they think differently when they're twenty-four than they do at fourteen! If they don't, then they're not developing the way they need to, and that's a bigger problem than the fact that they might change their minds a time or two.

But if that's true—if critical thinking is a natural, healthy part of human development—why do we feel so conflicted about it when it comes to our faith? Why are we so afraid of change in our beliefs? I wish I could've given myself more grace as my faith evolved. I've been on this journey for twenty years, so it was a gradual change in me. It wasn't a switch that was flipped overnight. It was more like a ship that started a slow turn in a different direction. The movements were so small that probably no one but me even realized it was turning. Looking back, I have so much grace for the girl trying to navigate those slow turns in her journey as her faith evolved. But at the beginning of this journey toward a growing and changing faith, the shifting of my beliefs was definitely a little scary.

Maybe it is for you too.

If that's the case, then let me pose a question: What if we don't have to be afraid? What if we could see this evolving faith as a normal part of our development? What if we could even see it as a good and necessary thing?

The good news? I think we can! But we have to start by reframing the way we see this process.

Deconstruction happens when something butts up against what you've thought to be true. And in case you haven't noticed, this happens a lot! Most American children grow up believing in Santa. It's a wild story about an old man who wears a red velvet suit, sneaks into our homes on Christmas Eve, and leaves presents under our trees. Because their parents present it to them as truth, they believe it. They embrace it. They hold on to it until their brains develop enough to question it. Then, at some point, they come to the realization that it's not true. In a sense, they've deconstructed their beliefs about Santa. The way they see Christmas has evolved.

Our faith is no different. Of course, I'm not suggesting that believing in Jesus is the same as believing in Santa Claus. I'm suggesting that deconstructing our beliefs is a process we walk through naturally and normally in other areas of our life. So why can't we do the same with our faith? Many childhood beliefs will be viewed and understood differently throughout our lives. Faith is really no different.

Many of us grew up believing that faith is about certainty. Are you certain you will go to heaven when you die? Are you certain that all things happen for a reason? Are you certain your prayers will be answered? Certainty is a huge selling point for Christians, and I understand why. We want to make sense of everything. We want to know why something happens. We want to feel sure about something—anything—in this life. Because certainty has a way of calming fear.

Certainty reinforced my faith at its start. I loved knowledge. That's why I read the Bible so much. I loved having all the answers. I even believed my interpretation of the Bible was the "right" one. (Don't we all go through this phase in our spiritual development?) But as my faith has grown, I've come to question whether certainty is the goal. I'm not sure that faith was ever supposed to be about whose interpretation is right or wrong. I'm not sure it was supposed to be based on certainty. After all, faith requires us to put our trust in something we can't see. I don't know about you, but I think that requires a level of getting comfortable with uncertainty. By "comfortable with," I mean we aren't surprised by uncertainty. We are comfortable saying, "I don't know and that's okay." We are fine with the fact that we aren't supposed to know everything (sorry to all my Enneagram 5s out there). Some things are certain—gravity is one of them. But when it comes to our faith, maybe we can find some joy in the mystery. I think that's what faith is supposed to be about. It's a process of discovering.

As I've walked this road of evolving faith, I've had to make friends with uncertainty. I've had to get comfortable with the not knowing. I've had to allow myself to adapt. My friend Pete Enns wrote a blog post about this very thing. In it he said, "Adaptation is not simply an acceptable dimension of faith—let alone a destructive influence. Rather, without adapting, faith cannot thrive and survive. A faith that does not adapt dies."[10]

This is what's at stake here. If we're not willing to give ourselves (and others!) the room to adapt and evolve in our faith, then we're putting the survival of that faith on the line. What will happen to our faith if we don't get comfortable wrestling with the uncertainty of it? Eventually, it won't remain at all.

Embrace Uncertainty

Today, the most common answer to questions about my faith is this: *I don't know.*

There is something freeing about being able to admit that sometimes I'm not sure. Sometimes I'm not certain. Sometimes I just don't know.

Of course, there's vulnerability in embracing our uncertainty. That's to be expected, as the opposite of certainty is vulnerability. To be vulnerable is to feel uncertain, and that's scary. Opening yourself up to the unknown can be downright terrifying.

But isn't standing in the unknown exactly what faith asks us to do? To trust in what we can't see? To step out even though we don't know what's coming? The Bible tells the story of Peter doing just that—stepping out to walk on water toward Jesus. That's what it means to embrace uncertainty.

If that's the case, then we need to give ourselves permission to follow where our faith leads. To step out in uncertainty. To let our faith evolve with honesty and vulnerability. To be okay with the possibility of winding up somewhere different from where we started.

The process isn't about a beginning or an end. It isn't even about a season or a short-term circumstance. It's just part of life. Shouldn't we all be growing, evolving, and changing? Shouldn't we all be taking note of our theology and raising it up against our experience to see if what we've been taught to be true actually is? Shouldn't we be comfortable with thinking critically about our faith?

I spent most of my professional life addressing this question: Why are teenagers graduating from high school and, consequently, their faith? The intent behind that question was to inform churches on how to teach kids about faith in such a way that they want to remain in that faith as they grow. What I've come to realize is that we've been asking the wrong question this whole time. Instead, we need to be asking, "How can we make space for teenagers—and all of us—to develop a faith of their own?" I wish people around me had asked themselves that question when I was a teenager. I wish I had been given permission to go on my own faith journey (wherever that may have led).

Give Yourself Permission

We all should give ourselves permission to develop a faith of our own. If we only ever believe what we were taught to believe simply because we were taught to believe it, that's not much of a faith. But if we allow ourselves to get in the ring and wrestle with our beliefs, then we can build something more authentic, more personal, and more lasting. Sure, the later in life we deconstruct, the more complicated it may be. By that point we have years of beliefs to untangle, but it's worth it.

So give yourself permission to evolve in your faith, even now. Don't rush it, not for the sake of your own comfort and not for the sake of anyone else.

Our family hasn't been in a church since the start of 2019. I'm writing this in 2023, and it's okay that we still don't go. We aren't ready yet. I've had conversations with friends about this very topic, and it seems like many people have found themselves in a similar position. The many reasons for not attending are unique to each person or family.

I'll tell you what I tell my friends. Usually the topic comes up loaded with a lot of guilt and shame. They tell me, "I really should go to church." My response is often a question: "Why do you feel like you should go to church?" If guilt or shame is driving the answer, then it's not a good reason to go back. My follow-up question is typically, "What are you missing in life that church would provide?" I think that helps evaluate whether you should go back. What are you looking for by attending church? Are you getting that anywhere else? Is there a church that will provide what you are looking for?

Church attendance has changed, especially since 2020. Most of us can get so much from experiencing church services online. We have endless sermons to consume. Countless songs to sing along to. And many Bible studies to participate in. And for many, community exists outside of church. So going back to a brick-and-mortar church building isn't necessary for them. And that should be okay.

In the South, going to church is a cultural thing. We live in a community that is heavy on church attendance. My girls' friends often criticize them for not attending church. But if we lived in another country, there may not even be churches to attend. Last time I checked, church attendance wasn't a requirement for faith. If your soul needs something that church provides, then follow that lead. But if guilt or shame is driving your desire to return, then I say to keep waiting. You have permission to wait. You have permission to evaluate. But you also have permission to return.

Stop Polling People

Maybe you know your faith is evolving. Maybe, like I did at the start, you've kept quiet about it because you're scared of what others will think. If that's you, let me give you a piece of advice I wish I'd taken myself: stop taking polls.

When we're scared, one of our first reactions is to poll the people around us.

Should I do this?

Is it okay I feel this way?

What do you think about this?

We want others to validate what we're feeling or processing. Maybe that will make us feel like we're on the right track. Maybe it will validate our own doubts or questions. Maybe it will convince us to stop going down this path. Whatever we're looking for, we hope to find it in the answers from others.

For many of us, polling has resulted in having a faith that isn't our own. We've let other people's opinions shape our beliefs. And where has that gotten us? Now we're sitting with a shaky sense of what we believe because it's based on what we've understood or lived out or believed for ourselves.

We need to build a faith of our own, and to do that, we can't only seek others' opinions. At some point, we need to ask *ourselves* questions instead of others: *Should I do this? Does this make sense to me? Does this line up with what I've experienced? Does this encourage connection or disconnection? Does this put me for others or against?*

Pay attention to the gut feeling that is pushing you to learn more. Do the work to ask yourself questions to build your own faith. What does that work look like? How do we widen the lens of our faith to build something of our own? Think about what you read, listen to, and watch and who you speak to. Read books from different perspectives. Even reading fiction has a way of widening your lens. You get to step into a different world and meet characters who aren't like you. It is a great way to flex the muscles of empathy and compassion. Listen to podcasts or sermons that aren't in the same line of thinking as your own. And spend some quality time with other people on a similar journey, asking them questions and allowing them to ask you questions as well.

Sit in the Gray

The longer I live, the more I realize just how much gray there is in life. I was confronted with this truth specifically as a new mother. I loved my child so much. But at the same time, I wanted to be away from her. I didn't know how to sit in the tension between the two. I felt like both couldn't be true—like I had to choose a side. I've come to realize that I didn't. Both can be true. I can love my daughter, and I can want to spend time away from her. Sometimes sitting in that tension is the healthiest balance I can have as a mother. I need time away from her, but that doesn't mean I don't want to be with her. But had I not learned to sit in that paradox, I might not have ever gotten comfortable there.

We need to find that same comfort in the gray when it comes to our faith. Yes, two opposite things can be true at the same time.

You can love God, and you can struggle with some of the Bible's teachings.

You can feel peace over where you are now while you grieve what you've lost to get here.

You can enjoy your child's presence while also wanting to hide in the bathroom to be alone.

You can feel peace over where you are now while you grieve what you've lost to get here.

We can hold the tension. Sitting in the gray reminds us that we are human and that this is a normal part of life.

Grieve It

For many of us, the evolving of our faith has been hard and painful. Not only have we lost relationships, but we've also lost, in some sense, the very thing that gave us meaning. In essence, we've lost some of our belonging.

If you have experienced this pain from an evolving faith, just know you are not alone. Know that many of us feel that same pain. I often tell Scott that the thing I grieve most is the loss of belonging. I've left jobs, left small groups, left churches, left friend groups. The hardest part in all of this is the loss. Sometimes we have to leave something because we no longer fit. Sometimes evolving means standing alone. It doesn't make others wrong. It just makes you different. And sometimes being different is lonely.

For our faith to evolve, we have to grieve what we've lost. We have to grieve the relationships, the jobs, the systems, the churches, and all the things that no longer seem to fit as our faith adapts and our lives change. We even have to grieve our loss of certainty to an extent. Then we have to get up and keep going. To find new ways of believing, of being, of growing in the faith we have now.

If you are feeling this, I want to share what has helped me get up and keep going in my own grief and questions.

- **Get outside.** I firmly believe you can experience God in nature. Step out onto the grass. Feel the breeze on your face. Move your body. Take in the view. Somewhere along the way, we elevated reading about

God above experiencing God. So if reading about God feels hard right now, go out and experience God instead.

- **Journal.** This one has been very helpful. I'm a writer, so maybe that's why, but there is something freeing about getting thoughts out of your head and onto paper. So as you process your evolving faith, put words around it. Your writing doesn't have to be clear or clean or concise. It doesn't have to be for public consumption. It just has to be for you—you and God and the faith journey you're on right now.
- **Have meaningful conversations.** This is absolutely necessary. I've been able to lean into a few people through this process—trusted and safe friends who hold no judgment. They don't fear when I say or suggest something wildly different. They don't try to convince me of or pressure me toward something else. They just show up, listen, and engage with me in a real, meaningful way. Consider who those people can be for you.
- **Experience art.** I mean art of all kinds! Museums or music or books. Read authors who help you feel like you're not alone (hopefully this book is that for you). Authors like Rachel Held Evans, Barbara Brown Taylor, and Pete Enns really helped me. Spiritual thinkers like Rob Bell and Peter Rollins broadened my perspective. And honestly, a little Taylor Swift never hurt anybody either! Find elements of faith in the books, music, and art you encounter.
- **Experience collective joy or grief.** If you've ever been to any sporting event, you've experienced collective joy. When the team runs onto the field and everyone

cheers? When fans jump to their feet when someone hits a home run? That's collective joy, and there is something deeply spiritual about it (even if it's in the context of a baseball game). But there is also something powerful about collective grief. That's what you may experience when you attend a funeral. The collective grief can be deeply spiritual. So lean into others who are evolving in the same way. Experience their joy and their grief. Ask them to do the same for you.

I think one of the fears in the faith community when it comes to evolving faith is that it means we'll abandon faith altogether. But the tighter we hold on because of fear the less room we give people to breathe. We can acknowledge the fear and then remember that tension is good. If we never felt tension, we would never wrestle with anything. Tension gives us the opportunity to reevaluate something, to test it. I think faith is bigger than any of us imagined. It's wider than we thought.

So when you lie awake at night wondering, "Do I still believe it?" take a breath and remind yourself that you're okay. This is normal. And more than that? It's good.

All of this is just part of living life. Looking back, I can see that I've been evolving in my faith my entire life. It's been growing and adapting all along and I didn't even know it. The gift in midlife is the freedom to look back less afraid. The questions of faith don't keep me up at night the same way they used to because now I know it's all part of the process. Faith was always meant to grow and develop. You have permission to be on a journey that is uniquely yours.

9
CHAPTER

why don't i feel like myself anymore?

I've lost my sparkle," I sighed. "My face used to light up, and I just don't feel like it does anymore. My hair used to have bounce, and it doesn't anymore. I used to be able to lose five pounds, and I can't anymore."

A friend in a similar stage of life nodded in agreement. By the time I finished my lament, I told her that I was just going to call my next book *I've Lost My Sparkle: Why Don't I Feel Like Myself Anymore?*

Because at night, when I toss and turn over my lost sparkle, I wonder,

Why don't I feel like myself anymore?

Friends in midlife, this is where we reside. We are solidly here. Midlife is real. Everything has changed, from our bodies to our jobs to our relationships. From what I've read, it's common to feel this way during this season of life. In fact, as many as 70 percent of women in this stage say they feel "invisible."[11] Do you know what happens when we feel invisible? Sometimes we withdraw. We say no to more social outings. We fear what people will think if we show up as our ordinary and unremarkable selves. The result? We miss out on important points of connection.

Did you ever judge those who were going through midlife crises? When I was in my twenties, young and full of answers, I wondered why people left their families or their careers or made rash decisions in this particular season. I thought something must be wrong with them. The truth is that I just hadn't faced what they'd faced. I hadn't been married for any length of time. I had never raised kids. I had never faced complacency or boredom in my job. I had never faced the death of a loved one. I had never faced feeling unknown to myself.

But then life moved forward. I found myself in the middle of life, married for nearly two decades, raising two teenagers. I also found myself ready to pivot in my work and discovered that much of what I had always believed had changed and evolved. Here in my own midlife, I'd be lying if I said I didn't get why people have midlife crises.

Not feeling like ourselves most certainly contributes to our unhappiness at this stage of life. And if we're scared to show up as the current version of ourselves—this seemingly unremarkable, unsparkly person we've become—we may pull back. We close off, we shut down, and ultimately, we get bored with our lives.

Of course, we don't necessarily feel our boredom. If someone walked up to us today and asked how we were doing, do you know how most of us would respond?

Busy.

Few of us would think to say we're bored. Because how can we be bored when we're so busy? How can we notice the complacency of this season if we've left no time in our schedules for it?

Back to school is always an extremely busy season for us, and I especially noticed it last year. The early mornings come back with a vengeance, and the fight to get my girls up, ready, and out the door on time begins all over again. Then activities start up and push into overdrive. Tennis season for middle school is in full swing, with plenty of matches and practices for Rory. Meanwhile, Sinclair is busy at the farm gearing up for her riding season. Plus, now that she's a high schooler, she has turned up the dial on her social life (which means I spend more time than normal in the car as her Uber driver). Honestly, everything feels like a blur. Even the weekends are full.

Yet even with all that busyness, somehow I've still felt bored.

I've found myself not really interested in anything. Nothing holds my attention. We'll sit down to watch something, but I'm just not interested. Often I want to go to sleep instead of hanging out with Scott in the evenings. Our schedule has fallen into a place where it's just sort of rinse and repeat. Sometimes I feel like I'm stuck at a certain pace, and that pace left me feeling lethargic.

Don't get me wrong! Sometimes boredom is good. Boredom can lead to creativity. (Go back and reread all the ways that creativity can combat comparison. If that's a struggle, then maybe you could use some boredom.) Books upon books are written to boost your creativity. In fact, I took a break from the podcast because I was seeking that sort of boredom. I wanted to boost my creativity. But the boredom I've been experiencing doesn't feel like the kind that is creating space for something new. It feels like an indication of something bigger.

Now, hear this: I'm not looking to make drastic decisions

or launch myself into a midlife crisis. But I am feeling quite restless. I am in a murky middle space in life and work. I feel busy yet bored. And I think we all know that busyness doesn't always equal fullness or happiness. A full schedule doesn't equal fullness. I could add more activities to my schedule, but I'm not sure that would remove the boredom I feel. I don't think it would help me feel like myself again.

Maybe you can relate. Maybe you feel like you are so busy that you can't catch your breath, yet you feel a strange boredom in your soul. Maybe you're up at night wondering who that girl is looking back at you in the mirror. You wonder why you don't feel like yourself anymore. I'm not sure what the answer to this seemingly stagnant season of midlife is, but I do know what it's not. I know the answer doesn't involve becoming busier. The answer isn't about finding a different job or a different relationship. The answer isn't about going from dull and boring to shiny and new.

Instead, the answer is sometimes found in asking the question.

Yes, that sounded very Yoda-like. What I mean is that maybe the answer looks different for each of us. But to find the answer, we have to ask questions about why we feel the way we feel:

What is underneath the feeling of boredom?
What am I trying to escape from when I just want to
     crawl into bed and go to sleep?
What happened that made me feel less like myself?
Is something missing from my life right now?

Asking those questions might bring a little clarity to next steps.

I have to remember that just as easily as this season rolled in, it will eventually roll out. But right now I can at least pay attention and reevaluate. Maybe that's part of what this season is for.

For asking why I do this or want this.

For getting curious about what I want in life now.

For saying no when I want to say no and yes when I want to say yes.

For finding my sparkle as the person I am now, not the person I was then.

Finding Your Sparkle Again

Now is the time to find our sparkle again. Just because it's currently missing doesn't mean it's gone for good.

That's a sentence I need to repeat to myself often: Just because it's missing doesn't mean it's gone for good. You know that to be true in other areas of life, so why can't it be true here? The other night, the Apple TV remote went missing. The search started with one kid, and then the search party grew to include the whole family combing the upstairs to find it. Do you know where we found it? You'll never guess (although, I bet you have similar findings in your own house). There was a lone boot on the floor of the common space. Inside the boot was the remote. Why? How did it get there? Who would think that was a good idea? All questions that lead you nowhere. We will never truly understand the mind of the teenager who put the remote in the boot. But we can understand the lesson it brings.

Just because something is missing doesn't mean it's gone.

So my challenge to you (and me) is to do something to bring the sparkle back. Go searching for it. Maybe that looks like splurging on skin care. (I did.) Or maybe you do something different with your hair. (I colored mine for the first time in twelve years.) Maybe it's taking a dance class or joining a book club. (I've found a lot of new hobbies in this season.) Maybe it's finally starting to strength train. (Lord knows we midlifers need to build muscle.) Whatever it is, do something that brings a little sparkle back.

I know these suggestions may feel like just surface-level fixes and that we need to address deeper issues during this season to understand why we feel the way we feel. Trust me, I'm working on those too (hello, therapy!). Some of us have been told that caring for things like our body, our hair, or our face is unimportant. That we shouldn't care about those things because that makes us superficial. Well, let me be the first to say it's okay. They're part of what make you, you. No, working out, fixing your hair, or getting a facial won't magically bring your old self back to life, but each of those things can help you feel good about who you are today. So give yourself permission to begin there. Sometimes addressing those surface-level things is the best place to start when it comes to finding our sparkle again.

Celebrate Your Progress

As you take steps toward finding your sparkle, celebrate the progress you make. You won't magically beat boredom and discover yourself overnight. Rather, it will happen one step, one moment, one decision, one thought at a time. Though the increments may be small, they're progress nonetheless, and progress isn't something to take lightly.

The other day, one of my girls came downstairs for breakfast before school. I noticed that her hair was curled and styled. She had really made some effort with the curling iron. As she entered the kitchen, she walked as if on a catwalk. Her confidence was apparent. With a toss of her hair, she said, "You know, it's amazing what your hair looks like when you wash it with shampoo."

I'm sorry . . . what?

"Wait, what do you mean?" I asked once I found the words to respond.

"Yeah, if you actually wash your hair with shampoo, your hair looks better," she confirmed.

"So, do you mean you *haven't* been washing your hair with shampoo all this time?"

A simple nod confirmed that, yes, my daughter in fact had not been washing her hair with shampoo!

Just letting you know that (a) I wasn't aware she wasn't using shampoo and (b) given that tweens and teens have such an aversion to hygiene, I'm going to count her discovery of the benefits of shampoo as a win.

It's a silly example. After all these years, she finally decided to use shampoo. It's a baby step, but a step nonetheless.

And isn't that what progress is?

Baby steps toward what's next.

Baby steps toward becoming.

Baby steps toward growth.

Baby steps toward a goal.

If we keep putting one foot in front of the other, we might look around and see that we made progress.

Baby steps are hard for someone like me who wants to get to the destination as quickly as possible. I want ten pounds to melt away after one workout. I want to become an expert without putting in the hours. I want to skip all the mundane or difficult parts to reach the end of the rainbow. I'd rather have giant leaps and bounds than baby steps because baby steps don't always feel like progress. That's when I have to remind myself that it's the process that counts. Remember, it's in the process that we find ourselves making progress.

So what are you baby-stepping toward? Take a minute today to celebrate your progress. No matter how small it is, notice it. Congratulate yourself for making progress.

Maybe you're trying to make healthy choices and you drank water today. That's a win.

Maybe you're trying not to be on social media and you refrained today. That's a win.

Maybe you're trying to be more positive and you held your tongue. That's a win.

Progress.

Baby steps.

Forward motion.

Take note of the progress you've made and walk with

the confidence of a teen girl who finally learned the value of using shampoo.

Wait for It

Some of us have been waiting quite some time for what's next, or for a solution, or for some relief. I wish there was a quick fix to waiting out this midlife moment, but there isn't. This is the hard part. It's not the answer any of us want to hear. The only way out is through, so if we want to feel like ourselves again, I think we have to wait. We have to show up, try something, and wait to see if it works.

The key for me in any kind of waiting is to remember that the wait won't last forever. My younger daughter got braces a few days ago. She doesn't like her teeth, so she had been anticipating and wanting braces for years. But do you know what happened when she finally got them? Of course you do! You've either had braces or raised someone who has had braces.

Pain.

Soreness.

Discomfort.

Her teeth ached. I had told her that nothing anyone said could help her truly understand what the pain would feel like. Everyone told her that she would be sore, but she didn't fully understand until she experienced it herself. I reminded her that the pain was temporary. That even though she'll have these on for a couple of years, this pain won't always be there. She just had to wait it out.

As I talked to her about that, I couldn't help but think about becoming a mother. That's another thing no one can adequately prepare you for. You know it will be painful in theory. You know that after you give birth you'll be tired. But you just can't know the extent of the pain and exhaustion until you experience it. But even though the process is painful, it doesn't last forever. The same is true for right now—you won't always feel this way.

Make Your Own Magic

One of my favorite books is *Big Magic* by Elizabeth Gilbert. I often return to it, especially in times when I feel a lack of inspiration or when I'm working on a creative project with a looming deadline.

The premise? We all have creativity—something magic—inside us just longing to get out. In the book, she paints a great word picture of what it looks like to keep that magic inside of us. She says it's like keeping a dog who's made to run and play locked up in the house all the time. It may start off fine, but eventually that dog will do something destructive to get its energy out. It might eat the couch! She writes,

> I firmly believe that we all need to find something to do in our lives that stops us from eating the couch. Whether we make a profession out of it or not, we all need an activity that is beyond the mundane and that takes us out of our established and limiting roles in society (mother,

employee, neighbor, brother, boss, etc.). We all need something that helps us forget ourselves for a while.[12]

Think about that. How have you been eating the couch? Going stir crazy? Feeling bored yet busy? Looking for your sparkle? Dying to feel like yourself again? Maybe instead of hoping creativity just comes to us, we need to get out there and try to find it ourselves!

For the last few years, I've been reading more books. Ironically, when I was a child, reading wasn't something I enjoyed. For a fourth-grade reading project that included a speech, I read a short book titled *Sleepy Dog*, which is basically a book for early readers. My mom still doesn't let me live that one down! As an adult, I decided that if I was going to read, it had to be for work—either for my actual job or for bettering myself. For a while, I read only the Bible and Bible studies, since those provided a way to better myself in my job and in my life. Still, reading felt like a chore. I must have equated reading with work because that's what learning in school always felt like.

Something started to change in 2016. I picked up a book that wasn't the Bible, a Bible study, or even about the Bible. I picked up *Rising Strong* by Brené Brown, and I was forever changed. Sure, this book was still on the theme of bettering myself, but it opened my eyes to other books. Within a couple of years of reading books like that, I found myself wanting to read stories and fiction. I realized there is so much good in getting lost in a story. Fiction expands my world by introducing me to people I may never have met. These stories increase my capacity for empathy and compassion and broaden my perspective. Now reading is a life-giving outlet for me. My husband lovingly calls me a book nerd, and I wear that title as a badge of honor.

That's one thing that has brought some magic back into this season of my life.

Have Fun

One of my family's favorite shows is *Justified*, featuring the character Raylan Givens, a US Marshal. Man, oh man. If you've seen this show, then you know. But I digress. There's one scene where Raylan is questioning a woman in the hill country of Kentucky. As they sit down, she pours a glass of whiskey, but it happens to be morning. He brings the time of day to her attention, and she responds, "Everybody's gotta have a hobby," and then sips the drink. Scott and I have laughed about that line over and over. No judgment here if drinking is your hobby (I certainly don't recommend it), but the point is right. Everybody does in fact need a hobby. We need to do something with ourselves. We need to remember that what made our lives happy and meaningful as children hasn't changed now in midlife—we still need to play. We still need to be creative in some way. Otherwise, we will be like what Elizabeth Gilbert described as someone eating the couch. We will find ourselves busy but bored.

A hobby can be anything that you find fun or relaxing or entertaining. It gives your hands and brain something to do. Somewhere along the way, I think hobbies got a bad rap. We sometimes feel like it is wasted time. I wonder if we make that assumption because our culture values work, productivity, and money more than it values fun. Scott recently decided to get into photography. He purchased a camera that is older than me and the equipment needed to develop his own film. He makes time in the evenings or on weekends to capture something and develop it. It's been a way to flex a creative muscle and incorporate fun into his daily life. And I decided to get back into tennis. I've started playing with Rory and some local women. Each week, I show up at the neighborhood park and spend time having fun. Why is it important, especially during this in-between season, to develop some hobbies? Because having fun is seriously important. Researchers say we are living in a fun drought. According to research, 97 percent of people wish they had more fun. For adults, 60 percent feel their life is too grown up and 73 percent miss aspects of childhood.

According to Dr. Emma Seppälä, a Stanford University expert on the science of happiness, emotional intelligence, and social connection, injecting small, incremental amounts of fun into your daily life reduces stress. She says, "If we focus on boosting fun and happiness in our lives, even in little ways, research suggests we can end up more productive, charismatic, energetic and innovative."[13] Play and fun have the ability not only to reduce our stress but also to build connection. Research shows that play serves as a way to bond with people.[14]

Pickleball is the fastest-growing sport in the United States. When I show up to play tennis, the pickleball courts are packed to the brim. It's not a surprise, given that the number of people playing this sport has increased over 150 percent over the last three years.[15] Everyone I know who plays has raved about how fun it is, so I had to see for myself. I didn't know anything about the sport, so I signed up for a local pickleball clinic and was hooked immediately. It's a sport that nearly everyone of any age or stage of life can play. Because of that, I convinced Scott to try it. After one session, he was hooked too. Now we go play pickleball twice a week. We're having fun together. The fun we have together playing this sport with a silly name builds our connection.

We put a lot of time, effort, and money into fun for our children, but many of us have forgotten to create fun for ourselves. We know it's important for our kids. We see the benefits in developing a skill. And we see the ways that sports or activities give them an opportunity to connect with others. Those are all good things—good things that we adults need too.

I think we feel guilty for having fun. We have prioritized work (and understandably so—we all need to pay our bills). But we've forgotten that a huge part of being human is having fun. And maybe we feel guilty for the money some hobbies cost. As with most things, when it comes to time and money, we simply need to evaluate our priorities and see how to make it work.

Maybe some of us are afraid of being judged. We might worry that someone will think less of us for taking time away from our family for ourselves, that we might look selfish. That is a mindset we have to fight against. I know I'm a better version of me when I do something for myself. When I work out, when I read a book, or when I play tennis, I'm better for it—and so is my family.

When it comes to fun, we have to plan for it. Most of us aren't having fun because we think fun has to be spontaneous. It doesn't. We've already established that our lives in this season are busier than ever. When life is busy, it's nearly impossible to have fun if we just wait for it to happen. Build fun—a little magic—into your schedule.

Not only do we need hobbies, but we need things to do for pleasure. Think about what you love—what brings you pleasure—and start there. A few months ago, I joined a good friend of mine for dinner. Our husbands were out of town, so we decided to try a new place. We ordered a bottle of wine to share, a cheese board, french fries, and brussels sprouts. We picked everything that sounded delicious, even if it didn't make sense on paper as a complete meal. Do you know what it felt like to eat the foods that sounded good to us? Pleasure. We need to incorporate into our lives things that delight our souls. We need to make our own magic as we try to feel like ourselves again.

Along with experiencing things for pleasure, we need to do things we are good at. Doing something we are good at incites a feeling of gratification. We need both pleasure and gratification to feel good about life. Some of us feel buried in our responsibilities, whether in work or home life. When we find ourselves deep in those seasons of life, we need to explore opportunities to do something that gratifies. You don't have to change jobs or get rid of your family. Those need to stay. But we can find some ways, maybe small ways, to do something that gratifies.

Maybe it's volunteering at your child's school office because you love to organize. Maybe it's working at a retail store part-time because you love retail. My family owns a wedding venue, and I started helping out on occasion. I meet with potential brides to show them the property, and some weekends I work at the wedding. I'm good at talking to people and love making people feel seen. This is a way to do that. It's gratifying.

As you lie awake at night trying to reconcile the girl you were and the girl you are now, just remember this season isn't the end. I know this not because I've lived through it—I'm still right in the thick of it with you! I know because I've watched other women in midlife rising up around me. Their self-discovery in this phase should be encouragement for all.

Have fun. Do something that reminds you of yourself. Do something that brings a sense of gratification. Do something for the sheer pleasure of it. Just because something is missing doesn't mean it's lost.

We can have hope that a lot more sparkle is out there waiting for us.

what can i do to ease my stress?

Every day, I take a walk with my dog, Murray. If you read my first book, then you'll remember two things about this activity. One, I call my daily walks "smoke breaks." I feel like we all need a reason to step outside and take a few deep breaths, much like someone who feels the need to take an actual smoke break at work. And two, I refer to my dog, Murray, as the greatest regret of 2017. While I still hold that to be mostly true, I have warmed up quite a lot to him. Now that I don't have to wrangle him onto a leash for walks, I enjoy him more.

Something I didn't share previously about those smoke breaks is that I spend time on the Marco Polo app to chat with friends as I walk. Okay, so I chat with only about three friends on this app. But one of them I chat with almost daily. She and I are very similar. In Enneagram speak, we share wings. I'm a wing 4, and she's a wing 3, so we understand each other's feelings and motivations. Both of us would be described as driven people, people who have worked hard and achieved quite a bit. So it's interesting that for us two midlifers, our conversations center on one thing: overwhelm.

I am tired. I have pushed hard in a lot of areas for a long time. Now in midlife I'm realizing how worn out—how burned out—I am. When I hit the bed at night, I often find myself awake and overwhelmed. And in the quiet of the night, I wonder,

What can I do to ease my stress?

Identify and Let Go

Before we go any further, I'd ask you to pause and consider this: What is causing your stress? What is causing your overwhelm?

Think about what adds stress to your life. If you're feeling bold, write those things down! Of course, keep in mind that each thing that lands on your list is not necessarily all bad. Your kids, your job, the changes you're facing in this season, your marriage, your relationships, the to-do list—these on their own are not the enemy of your peace. But how you manage them may be. Sometimes avoiding or hiding from the stress seems easier than easing it. Out of sight, out of mind. Sometimes that looks like numbing the stress—overeating, undereating, drinking too much, shopping too much, working too much, watching too much. But there's a better way.

Once you've got your burnout list on paper, take an honest look at it. Out of all the things stressing you out, what can go? What can you delegate? What can you remove from your plate? You may have to get creative in the way you answer those questions. I'm certainly not suggesting you quit your job, or abandon caring for your kids, or walk away from your marriage simply because you're in a season of stress. What I am suggesting is when you're in a state of overwhelm, something has to give, and it's up to you to creatively and honestly consider what that is.

Maybe it's not hosting the family event at your house this year.

Maybe it's not signing up to be room mom.

Maybe it's not taking on another animal (or two horses!).

Maybe it's saying no to one more extracurricular activity for your kid.

Maybe it's letting go of a relationship.

Maybe it's letting go of a belief.

What can you get rid of to bring a little more peace to your life? What can you do about your own overwhelm?

Complete the Stress Cycle

I'm learning a lot of tangible ways to help with my overwhelm. One of the most helpful books has been *Burnout: The Secret to Unlocking the Stress Cycle* by sisters Emily Nagoski and Amelia Nagoski. In their book, they talk about the need for us to complete the stress cycle. In other words, our bodies need to physically work out the stress. We need to do something to move the stress through our system and out of our body. We need to learn to speak the language of our bodies. And how do bodies speak? By doing something physical (enter my daily smoke breaks!). This doesn't have to be a walk around the block with your dog and your friends (via app). It could be anything from deep breathing or laughter to crying or dancing or running. I've recently convinced Scott that we need a treadmill at home. Just like the rest of us, he carries a lot of stress. I have been the local evangelist for the need to move the stress out of our bodies in a physical way. He finally tried it for himself. He hopped on the treadmill, set the pace and timer, and began to walk. By the end of a week of walking every day, he saw the value. And now at the end of a workday, he steps on the treadmill to move the stress through his body. He's learning the way to speak to his body in a way it will understand. Whatever activity you choose—and it could be different on any given day—the point is to do something, anything, that releases the stress from your body.

This year, I've grown to hate one thing in my life with a fiery passion. Like, I have an I-want-to-throw-plates-against-a-wall hatred toward it.

And that's gnats.

They are the worst. Worse than spiders. Worse than flies. Worse than mosquitoes (hot take). They are in your business, pestering, and it's downright rude.

I don't know if there are more gnats because we live in the country or maybe this part of Tennessee is just infested with them, but we've never had an issue with gnats before now. It feels like they have taken over my home! Upon returning from our vacation recently, I walked into my house to find the gnat situation out of control. As I was cooking dinner that night, I was under full-blown attack. Everywhere I turned, those pesky gnats were in my business.

I opened the trash, there they were.

I opened the silverware drawer, there they were.

I chopped lettuce, there they were.

Just telling you about this now is raising my blood pressure.

I was so upset, stressed, and overwhelmed that I nearly shattered all the plates in my vicinity. And while that would have felt nice and probably relieved some stress, I know that being destructive would only make the situation worse in the long run. So I did something else instead.

I asked for a hug.

Cue Keith Anderson's song "Somebody Needs a Hug" because that somebody was me! I literally yelled up the stairs where my girls were and said, "Can somebody please come give me a hug?!"

Maybe asking for a hug seems strange to you. It would never have crossed my mind before, but after reading *Burnout*, I thought it was worth a try. Research suggests that a twenty-second hug releases stress and tells the body that it is safe. That type of hug is just long enough to nearly feel awkward, but hugging someone you love and trust signals security, and that security helps you let go of stress. What a simple thing we can give and receive when we feel stressed or when our partner or kids feel stressed!

(And as for the gnat situation, I am in full warrior mode and will annihilate them all. Gnats, if you are reading, you have been warned.)

Buck It Out

I was never one who enjoyed roller coasters growing up. In fact, everything about theme parks scared me as a child. I was once petrified by a large Papa Smurf character at the state fair. Why do church youth groups always want to take students to places like Six Flags? Every time, I would put on a brave face, climb into the roller coaster, and hold my breath as we exited the safety of the platform.

It's no surprise that, as an adult, I don't like roller coasters in relationships. Unfortunately, this is what raising teenagers is. It's like being trapped on an emotional roller coaster—one from a horror movie. You can never get off of it. You just have to keep riding the ride, over and over again.

This year our oldest entered high school. Our small town has open enrollment, so families can choose where to send their kids to school. In theory, this is great. Who doesn't like to have choices? Well, in actuality, it's terrible. I just want to go where we are zoned. Having too many choices leaves room for drama, fear, and anxiety.

We spent a year processing where to send her before finally making the call. The bad news? The choice we made was opposite of what my daughter wanted to do. Since the day we told her, she's put us all on an emotional roller coaster. One day she's fine with it. The next day she feels like her life is over. After that, she's fine again. And the cycle continues.

During this roller coaster with my daughter, we watched *The Horse Whisperer*. In it, Robert Redford is the horse whisperer himself, hired to help a young girl and her horse get back to riding after a traumatic accident.

In the film, the traumatized horse needs the opportunity to buck it out. It needs to have a safe place to work out the emotions stemming from the accident—the fear, the anxiety, the pain. All the while, as the horse bucks it out, the horse whisperer just stands there, quiet but present. He doesn't fight back. He doesn't buck back. He waits for the horse to run its course and then come to him.

I may not be the teen whisperer, but this is exactly what happened with my daughter. She bucked it out over this school decision. For nearly an hour, she was wild with emotion over it. Then she ran to her room, cried some more, and called a friend. I just stood by and let her be. I didn't correct, I didn't console, and I didn't dare even approach a teenager in such a state. I'm no fool! Instead, I just gave her space to buck it out.

Eventually, just like the horse in the movie, she returned. She walked over and apologized for screaming. Then she crawled into my arms on the sofa. Bucking it out didn't fix all her problems or ease all her fears about going to a new school, but it did give her space to get the stress out of her system, to release what was causing her overwhelm.

Friends, maybe we need to do the same. I'm not suggesting a temper tantrum (though maybe that wouldn't hurt once in a while). But I am suggesting you give yourself space to work out your stress in a way that works for you.

Maybe it's phoning a friend to lament.

Maybe it's taking a day off to shut down and feel the emotions.

Maybe it's journaling, or working out, or crying it out.

Whatever it looks like for you, find a way to buck stress out of your system.

Take a Vacation from Your Problems

Up until this year, I'd never taken a trip by myself for rest or retreat. Sure, I've gone on work trips and stayed in a hotel alone, but it wasn't technically a retreat. But as I write this now, I'm in a hotel room on a retreat—alone. What sort of retreat? you might ask. A retreat from my kids, from my life, from responsibilities, from everything that is overwhelming me in this season of life. I can't help but think about one of my favorite movies, *What about Bob?* Bob's psychiatrist prescribes him a vacation from his problems. Well, today I am Bob, and this is basically the purpose of my retreat.

Taking a trip like this never really crossed my mind, partly because I've always felt like I "shouldn't" do it. I shouldn't spend the money. I shouldn't leave the kids. I shouldn't leave all the responsibility on Scott. I shouldn't take so much time just for me. But I also didn't think about going away alone because, if I'm honest, I don't like being alone. My husband, on the other hand, dreams of taking trips alone. He once took a ten-day trip to gather some video footage in Hawaii and Las Vegas. While he was away, we rarely spoke because of the time difference. When he returned, I had never seen him happier. He reveled in not speaking to anyone that whole time. I feel like I would have turned into Tom Hanks's character in *Cast Away* after day one. Don't get me wrong—I love having pockets of alone time, like taking a thirty-minute walk, or reading a book while taking a bath, or driving a couple of hours in the car. I usually need only a couple of hours of alone time to feel recharged. But days? To me, that feels unsettling.

One morning after the girls left for school, Scott brought up the suggestion for me to finally take this retreat. He looked at me and simply said, "I think you need to go." He had been watching the stress and burnout overload me. He knew I was at a breaking point (or maybe he knew I was well past the breaking point). He knew that to get out of my overwhelm, I needed to recharge. I agreed. How did I know I needed this extended smoke break? I felt off, like I wasn't fully myself. I found myself living right under the line of calm and togetherness, meaning if my kids did something annoying (like fighting), my tolerance and my ability to handle the situation well simply were not there. If someone cut me off while driving, I found myself almost in tears. If one more thing got added to my to-do list, I was going to snap. It was like I was in a constant state of fight or flight. I needed some time to come back to myself. I needed a time to let go of my responsibilities. I needed a grand smoke break.

Because Scott knows me so well, he also knew what I needed to recharge. Because I don't like being alone, I didn't need to go to a cabin in the woods. I didn't need to travel to a distant place. Instead, I needed to stay in a nice place with easy access to things and people I love.

A lack of connection contributed to my season of burnout. With our move, I'd been so busy managing everything in our lives that I don't think I realized how much I missed my people until I hit a breaking point without them. I had been knee-deep in launching my book, easing the girls' transition to their new schools, and making sure everyone around me was okay. But when the dust settled, I realized I was lonely. I went from seeing friends in person on the regular to seeing friends every so often. I missed my connections, and my husband saw it. So when he suggested this retreat, he proposed I take it in our former town so that I could connect with friends.

The idea that connection is essential to our healing process was highlighted when I listened to an episode of Jen Hatmaker's *For the Love* podcast. She interviewed Dr. Bessel van der Kolk, author of *The Body Keeps the Score*. In that conversation, he talked about how we are social creatures wired for connection. He gave the example of how yoga is good for the body but that it's even better if done in a class with others.[16] Adding the element of social connection helps the body even more. That's why my retreat away needed to include not only a break from responsibility and an opportunity to rest but also a chance to connect with friends.

Trust me when I tell you those few days at a nice hotel in the Atlanta area did wonders for my overwhelm. It was a chance to simply take care of myself. To give myself what I needed when I needed it. To remove myself from the daily stresses of life so that I could breathe and gain perspective before I returned to my regularly scheduled life.

A full, abundant life means taking care of myself. Finding rest. Connecting with people in person in real life.

The state I'd been living in—a state of burnout—didn't feel like a full life. A full, abundant life means taking care of myself. Finding rest. Connecting with people in person in real life. Not everyone can escape to a hotel for a few days, but what we can do is recognize where we are and when we need a retreat. Then we can find small ways to make that happen so that our smoke breaks, both simple and grand, can give us some rest.

Let It Go

I've always been pro therapy, though I hadn't gone much myself. I tried a counselor back in 2016 when I was going through an exceptionally hard season of life. Parenting young kids was hard. Scott had left the company he created to try something new. A close friend was mad at me for reasons I didn't understand. Even though my work seemed to be going well, everything else in my life felt hard. But when therapy was initially suggested, I didn't consider it an option.

I wasn't opposed to therapy. I was just opposed to the current state of my bank account. With Scott leaving his company, money was more than tight. Every month, bills were piling up. I was afraid we were drowning, and therapy isn't cheap. So when a friend suggested seeing a counselor through her church, which was a much cheaper option, I decided to give it a try.

I went two times and hated it. I didn't connect well with the counselor. Instead of compassion, I felt judgment and shame. She listened to my story and suggested I read the book *Boundaries* by Henry Cloud and John Townsend. Looking back, I can see why she suggested it; boundaries have never been my strong suit. But in that moment of pain, the suggestion didn't land. So I never went back.

I decided to handle it on my own. I did a few years of self-work: reading books, listening to podcasts, and incorporating some healthy daily rhythms into my life. That self-work worked for many years. I saw a lot of growth and change. I felt like I grew as a human. My heart expanded toward myself. But after a few years, I was in another hard season. By 2022 I knew I needed therapy. I could go only so far by myself. I needed help.

After I met with my therapist a couple of times and told her how I was feeling in this season, she met me with compassion. Finally, she said something I hadn't thought about before.

"You've experienced a lot of loss in this season. Moving, changes in your faith, loss of dreams. That's a lot to grieve," she gently suggested.

According to Brené Brown's research, the foundational elements of grief are loss, longing, and feeling lost.[17] Much of what we're overwhelmed by at this stage of life—midlife—is grief. We've experienced enough life to feel a sense of loss. Loss of dreams. Loss of what could be. Loss of what we thought we knew or understood about something or someone. We've experienced longing. Longing for what was. Longing for the body we once had. Longing for the way our relationships used to be. Longing for a different stage of parenthood. And we certainly know what it is to feel lost. We've worked for years striving toward a certain goal only to realize that it won't happen. We often feel like we've lost our sense of purpose. We're lost as to where to go or what to do next.

When my therapist brought up grief, I was shocked. I

didn't think I was grieving anything. But the more she had me talk, the more tears pricked my eyes. (And I hate crying in front of others!) In that moment in her office, I allowed myself to feel the loss.

I allowed myself to grieve.

Those feelings of grief, longing, and loss don't go away simply because we acknowledge them. It is a longer process than that. But we have to start by acknowledging those feelings. I had to deal with my grief.

In that process, I realized that with grief comes death. Before this, I only associated grief with actual death. I hadn't connected it to loss or longing. But as humans, we experience death in many ways beyond the physical. And just like with physical death, to process and move forward, we often need to bury something.

To process and move forward, we often need to bury something.

I had to let go of and bury my dream of being known on a large scale. I know that dream may sound a little self-absorbed, but it was real and shaped how I saw my life. I've craved the stage since I was little. I loved to perform, especially growing up. I lived for piano recital nights or opportunities to sing a solo at church. That desire to perform continued when I stepped into a career. Anytime I was given the opportunity to stand onstage at church with a microphone, my insides lit up. My dream as a college kid was to cohost a morning talk show, preferably with Regis Philbin. Maybe that sounds like a fame-hungry dream, but at the heart of it, I just liked performing. It was so much fun. Hosting my podcast and writing books were a part of the performance. I loved being known for being helpful.

But in midlife, something changed. My "performances" weren't being noticed like I hoped. Some would say my "performance" wasn't good enough. I realized that what I had been working toward and longing for wasn't going to happen.

Loss of a dream.

Longing for what was supposed to be.

Feeling lost and without a purpose.

Grief.

I had to allow myself to feel grief over these things. To be sad. To accept what didn't happen and would not happen. To let go of it, I first had to grieve it.

Here's what's interesting, though: with death comes rebirth. This is part of the design of our world! My family owns a wholesale nursery, so over seventy acres of trees, plants, and shrubs are just outside our house. In the summer, everything is full and colorful. But with fall, the leaves on the trees fall to the ground, and by winter, the trees go into a death of sorts. Then comes spring, when new life grows. That sounds a little cheesy, but it's true. When we grieve a loss—when we bury a dream or relationship—we make space to experience something else. When we let go, we're making way for something new.

I don't know what will be rebirthed. As I write, the trees are bare. We are in the dead of winter, but I can't help but feel hopeful. Spring will come for the earth, and spring will come for me. Something will be reborn in me. The grief will grow into something new.

What do you do while you are in the dead of winter in life? What do you do while you feel lost, sad, and full of grief? What do you do when those feelings overwhelm you?

Feel the loss. Feel the grief. Look for what will be reborn.

And don't do it alone! Invite someone into the grief that overwhelms you. Maybe it's a therapist, maybe it's a spouse or partner, maybe it's a friend, or maybe it's just the pages of your journal. Find a trusted person or safe space where you can be honest.

Find a trusted person or safe space where you can be honest.

All of us have experienced loss, longing, and a feeling of overwhelm in some form or fashion over the years. When you're brave enough to speak about your own experiences, you open the door for someone else to be brave too. I wouldn't be writing this book if I had never opened up to other people going through this same stage of life. Opening up not only helped me grieve, it also got me to the place where I could finally let go. And I believe it can do the same for you!

Make a Plan

Let's talk about what we can do when we feel stressed or overwhelmed, even what we can do regularly to avoid stress. What can you do daily, weekly, monthly, or yearly to give yourself what you need? I asked myself that question as I prepared to leave the comfortable retreat of a nice hotel and return to my regular life. Everything that overwhelmed me was still there. My responsibilities, the stress points, my grief—all still there. To face my life without taking a deep dive back into stress and burnout, I had to return with a plan.

When you're brave enough to speak about your own experiences, you open the door for someone else to be brave too.

My plan is to keep moving my body daily. That means getting in ten thousand steps daily. Weekly, I continue to work out at the studio in town. Not only does it do my midlife body good to lift weights, but it serves as a social connection point with others. I also build in a weekly connection point with a friend for a walk or coffee or lunch. Monthly, I schedule dates with Scott (ideally more than once a month!). And yearly, I hope to do a retreat again.

That's my plan to combat my overwhelm.

Now think about your plan. What is it that you need? What might help you find some peace? What might keep you from feeling so overwhelmed? Come up with your plan, and then ask for it. No one can give you what you need if you don't articulate it.

To get you started, here are a few ideas you could incorporate into your plan:

Take a nap.
Enjoy a mindful shower or bath.
Try a guided meditation.
Read a book.
Go for a walk.
Unclench your jaw.

Pull your shoulders down.
Turn off your phone.
Stretch.
Have a good cry.
Share a meal with a friend.
Take a trip.

If you feel how I felt, you're not alone. You're not strange for grappling through burnout and overwhelm. It's normal. We carry so much stress, and often we are terrible at taking care of ourselves. We put ourselves at the bottom of the list. But I know that when I'm in a healthier state of mind, I am better toward everyone, including those closest to me and myself! That's why taking care of ourselves is important. I know that you, too, want to be your best self. I know you want to find peace in place of overwhelm. I know you want to find the life of abundance you are meant to live. Because when you do, you'll sleep peacefully again, both in midlife and beyond.

conclusion

When You Still Can't Sleep

Writing this book has felt deeply personal. Not that the previous books weren't personal; they were. I've tried to put my finger on it—on why this one felt different. I think it's because I felt like I was writing this book in real time.

Now, I'm glad I wrote it when I did. I'm glad I pushed myself to step into this raw, vulnerable space. I am often reminded from you, dear reader, that you feel seen when I write or speak on a podcast. You feel like someone understands your thoughts and puts words to what you are thinking and feeling. For that reason, stepping into this space was good, for me and hopefully for you too.

I have raised a lot of questions in this book. They're questions I believe you are already asking. Or maybe questions you now feel you have permission to ask. Unfortunately, this book won't keep you from waking up in the middle of the night. We truly have biology to thank for that. Our bodies will still wake us. Our minds will still wonder. Our nights will still be messy from time to time.

Here's what gives me hope. Whatever we're going through—whatever wakes us in the night—won't always be this big. Sleepless nights won't always be a struggle in our lives. When Sinclair was a newborn, we had a monitor in our room even though her room was next door. Trust me, I could hear her clearly without a monitor. Like clockwork, she would awake in the night ready to be fed. I remember the first morning I woke up without being awakened by her in the middle of the night. I have never jumped out of bed faster than I did that morning—I thought she was dead or missing! What else would explain a full, quiet night's sleep? I raced to her room and busted through the door, and there she was sound asleep. And just like that, the season of feeding her in the middle of the night was over.

I tell you this to say that this season will pass. Sleepless nights won't always be your present or your future. I still wake most nights around 3:00 a.m., but I spend fewer nights with questions and worries whirling around and around in my head as I've put some of what I'm learning into practice. I hope the same becomes true for you.

To help you with that, do some work during the daylight hours. Take each of these chapters and dig a little deeper. Go chapter by chapter if you want. When I started this process, I started with my feelings. I listed out everything I felt. It was a long list, and that's okay! We have to start with being honest about what we feel. Feelings aren't wrong; they aren't the enemy. They are indicators of what's going on inside, and that means we need to give them proper attention.

Then get curious about those feelings. Ask questions like:

Why do I feel this way?
What could be causing this fear, this jealousy, this
    sadness?
What do I need?

I truly believe that asking questions—being curious—is the avenue for growth. I want to be someone who keeps growing and evolving, and curiosity is how this happens. Let your curiosity guide you to discover more about yourself, more about where you are in life, and more about what you need.

It's frustrating to lie awake and have your body refuse to cooperate and fall back asleep. And I know sometimes, when you're watching the clock tick closer and closer to morning and sleep still hasn't come, all the curiosity in the world won't help. So as we wrap up our time together, let me get practical. A good portion of this book deals with topics and theory, but I also want to give you some easy things to try when you can't sleep.

First of all, *normalize that you are struggling to sleep.* Sometimes I just need to remind myself that this is normal, that everyone goes through days or seasons of sleeplessness. Normalizing it helps me take the pressure off. Next, *step out of scarcity mode.* When I'm awake at night and glancing at the clock to see only fifteen minutes have gone by since the last time I checked, it's easy to move from stressing about my kids to stressing about the lack of sleep.

I start doing the math on how much sleep I will get if I can fall asleep right at that second. Then I think about how crappy the day ahead will be because of the lack of sleep. I just go round and round the scarcity wheel. To stop myself from taking that ride again, I say, "It's gonna be okay. You may be tired, but you can get coffee." Coffee really does solve most of my problems (am I right or am I right?).

After normalizing it and stepping away from scarcity, try a few of these tactics that have helped me on many a sleepless night.

- **Breathe.** I know that might sound childish, but it works. I take slow and intentional breaths in through my nose and out through my mouth. I slowly count to four with each breath. Breathe in for one, two, three, four. Breathe out for one, two, three, four. Breathing helps to regulate my mind. It reminds my brain and signals to my body that I can relax and go to sleep.
- **Write it down.** Sometimes I just need to write something down. You can keep some paper and a pen by your bed or send an email to yourself like I do. I can't tell you how many emails I receive from myself in the middle of the night. I worry that I'll forget whatever I'm thinking about, so simply writing it down sometimes removes the anxiety.
- **Watch or listen to something.** Okay, this is tricky. You don't want to watch something that engages your mind. You want to watch something that doesn't require much attention. I used to watch *What about Bob?* or *You've Got Mail.* I know those movies by heart.

Now I watch *Hart of Dixie*. I've seen that show a million times at this point. I can close my eyes in the middle of the night and listen to the show without feeling the need to engage in it. I set a timer on my phone to shut it off after thirty minutes. After a while, I almost always fall asleep. It's enough to distract my brain from all the things it felt like it needed to think about at 3:00 a.m.

- **Eat something.** Lastly, sometimes I just need to eat something. When Sinclair was six and going through a season of sleeplessness, the doctor suggested that she eat a spoonful of peanut butter before bed. She thought it might help her blood sugar not to bottom out in the middle of the night and thus wake her up. I sometimes try that trick myself. If I feel hungry before bed, I'll eat a spoonful of peanut butter in hopes of not waking up. Or if I wake in the night and feel hungry, I allow myself to eat a spoonful of peanut butter and then go back to bed.

These ideas may not work for you, but they are in my tool kit for restless nights. Maybe along the way you'll find a few new tricks that work for you too. My hope for all of us is more restful nights with our heads against our pillows and peace permeating our minds.

At the beginning of the book, I talked about how Sinclair went through a "scared at night" phase when she was little, with her own Rolodex of fears that she cycled through each night. I mentioned how we worked during the daylight hours to come up with a game plan so that when Sinclair woke, she'd know what to do. Well, this book contains my Rolodex of fears—my list of what keeps me awake at night. But also, these chapters have become my game plan, a guide for what to do when the fears, worries, and anxieties of life wake me.

I hope they do the same for you.

I hope you take this guide and work through it.

I hope you come up with your own game plan.

Now, let me leave you with one last piece of advice: *Don't do it alone.* I know that is sometimes easier said than done. You don't need a long list of friends; you just need one. One person you can reach out to and connect with on a regular basis. One person to encourage you toward peace of mind and rest in truth. One person to help you stay connected. We are social beings created to do life with other humans. I know sometimes it feels safer to keep all our feelings tucked inside, to not voice those feelings, concerns, and questions out loud. But every time I've shared these things with a trusted person (friend, partner, or therapist), the weight of them feels lighter. The peace comes sooner. The sleep comes easier.

So before your head hits the pillow for one more night, find someone to connect with about whatever is plaguing your sleep. Will it fix your sleeplessness right away? Probably not. But it will help, even if only a little over time. After all, everything is better with a friend.

Even our sleepless nights.

notes

1. Brené Brown, *The Gifts of Imperfection* (Center City, MN: Hazelden, 2010), 97.
2. Jack Feuer, "The Clutter Culture," *UCLA Magazine*, July 1, 2012, https://newsroom.ucla.edu/magazine/center-everyday-lives-families-suburban-america.
3. *Hope Floats*, directed by Forest Whitaker (Los Angeles, 20th Century Fox, 1998).
4. "Loneliness and the Workplace," Cigna, 2020, https://www.cigna.com/static/www-cigna-com/docs/about-us/newsroom/studies-and-reports/combatting-loneliness/cigna-2020-loneliness-factsheet.pdf.
5. Daniel A. Cox, "The State of American Friendship: Change, Challenges, and Loss," Findings from the May 2021 American Perspectives Survey, American Survey Center, June 8, 2021, https://www.americansurveycenter.org/research/the-state-of-american-friendship-change-challenges-and-loss/.
6. Emma Seppälä and Marissa King, "Burnout at Work Isn't Just About Exhaustion. It's Also About Loneliness," *Harvard Business Review*, June 29, 2017, https://hbr.org/2017/06/burnout-at-work-isnt-just-about-exhaustion-its-also-about-loneliness.
7. "How to Make Friends? Study Reveals Time It Takes," University of Kansas, March 28, 2018, https://news.ku.edu/2018/03/06/study-reveals-number-hours-it-takes-make-friend#:.
8. "Elizabeth Gilbert: Curiosity and the Passion Fallacy. [Best Of]," *Good Life Project* podcast, August 21, 2017, https://

notes

shows.acast.com/61de0665cc27c20014ea15cf/episodes
/elizabeth-gilbert-curiosity-and-the-passion-fallacy-best-of.

9. Jonathan Haidt, *The Happiness Hypothesis: Finding Modern Truth in Ancient Wisdom* (New York: Basic, 2006), 223.

10. Pete Enns, PhD, "Progressive No More: Brief Thoughts on Adaptive Christianity," Bible for Normal People, April 29, 2022, https://thebiblefornormalpeople.com/progressive -no-more-brief-thoughts-on-adaptive-christianity/.

11. "Invisibility in Later Life," Gransnet, accessed August 28, 2023, https://www.gransnet.com/online-surveys-product -tests/feeling-invisible-survey.

12. Elizabeth Gilbert, *Big Magic* (New York: Riverhead, 2015), 172.

13. "Chase Freedom Unlimited Card Survey Reveals a 'Fun Gap' in America," Business Wire, April 8, 2016, https:// www.businesswire.com/news/home/20160408005471/en/ Chase-Freedom-Unlimited-Card-Survey-Reveals-a-.

14. Meredith Van Vleet, Vicki S. Helgeson, and Cynthia A. Berg, "The Importance of Having Fun: Daily Play among Adults with Type 1 Diabetes," *Journal of Social and Personal Relationships* 36, no. 11–12 (November 2019): 3695–710, https://doi.org/10.1177/0265407519832115.

15. "Pickleball Popularity Statistics and Demographics: Facts & Infographic," Pickleball Player, March 17, 2023, https:// thepickleballplayer.com/pickleball-popularity-statistics -demographics-infographic/.

16. Dr. Bessel van der Kolk and Jen Hatmaker, "Your Body Keeps the Score: Unwinding Trauma with Dr. Bessel Van Der Kolk," episode 07, in *For the Love* podcast, produced by Jen Hatmaker, https://jenhatmaker.com/podcasts /series-38/your-body-keeps-the-score-unwinding-trauma -with-dr-bessel-van-der-kolk/.

17. Brené Brown, *Atlas of the Heart* (New York: Random House, 2021), 110–12.

A Mother's Guide to Raising Herself

What Parenting Taught Me About Life, Faith, and Myself

Sarah Bragg

For any mom who has ever felt inadequate, overwhelmed, or guilty in trying to balance it all, popular podcaster Sarah Bragg offers brilliant clarity and respite in this friendly manual for becoming your most authentic self, instead of just surviving motherhood.

It's easy to lose our sense of self in the all-consuming process of raising our children, but Sarah reminds us that the best gift we can bring to our kids is our true, authentic selves. Through vulnerable and relatable stories, no-nonsense wisdom, and a compassionate perspective for all the joys and challenges of motherhood, Sarah provides shame-free practical help to surviving right where you are in life, in relationships, in work, and in faith.

This guidebook to health and sanity for the wilderness of parenting will help you:

- Give yourself permission and find the courage to show up as yourself
- Wrestle with how purpose, work, and calling fit together
- Notice and celebrate the good that's happening right around you
- Remember your worth is not in your kids or your role as a parent but in something far more lasting

Find solidarity, understanding, and helpful encouragement to embrace all that motherhood is and remember who you truly are. Because you matter, and raising great kids starts with raising yourself well.

Available in stores and online!

From the Publisher

GREAT BOOKS

ARE EVEN BETTER WHEN THEY'RE SHARED!

Help other readers find this one:

- Post a review at your favorite online bookseller

- Post a picture on a social media account and share why you enjoyed it

- Send a note to a friend who would also love it—or better yet, give them a copy

Thanks for reading!